Also by James Castagno

*Octavia and the Greek Key*

*Lady of the Lantern*

*Dance of the Red Panel*

**Witness to Terror**
Fugitive Series Book One

*Out of Tunis*
Fugitive Series Book Two

# Out of Naples

## Fugitive Series Book Three

## James Castagno
### A Novella

*Out of Naples* is a work of fiction. All characters, businesses, places, events or incidents either are the products of the author's imagination or are used fictitiously. Any resemblance to actual persons, living or dead, or actual events and locales is purely coincidental.

*When you have to kill a man, it costs nothing to be polite.*

–Winston Churchill

## *Chapter I*

## *HOME*

U.S. Marshal Service Chief Inspector Joe Costa sat at his desk in the Rome U.S. Embassy. He gazed at the small cardboard box he had received in a diplomatic pouch. Three weeks earlier, the U.S. Attorney's office in the Southern District of New York asked the Italian government for their assistance. The Rome Embassy received a copy of their request and forwarded it to the Italian Ministry of Justice. He smiled as he picked up the German-made switchblade lying beside the box and pressed the lever, allowing the polished Solingen steel blade to spring open.

With his thumb and index finger holding the tip of the blade, he guided it along the tape securing the package. Inside lay three sealed espresso pods. He removed one, stared at the wrapper and began to rip it open, but stopped. *Five hundred and sixty dollars, I'll wait for the meeting.*

When his cell phone rang, he dropped the packet into the box, tapped the screen and the speaker icon. "Pronto."

"What do you mean pronto? Only Italians answer their phone that way and you saw it's me," his wife Nina said.

"True, but one of my passports is red, and Italian Republic is printed on the front cover."

"How does it feel being a man with two countries?"

*Actually good.* The embassy restricted his travel to places in Eastern Europe and Southwest Asia. Americans needed to be cautious, and travel was less risky on a European Union passport. "The same as it did when I had one. Today I'm here, and next week you and I will be in New York City."

"That's why I called," Nina said. "How long are we going to be there? Sofia asked Angelo, but he couldn't tell her. We both need to plan what clothes we'll take."

"Anything you pack will do, as long as it is sexy."

"The lingerie is already in the suitcase, but it would be nice to know how to dress when we leave the hotel. I want to see the Statue of Liberty and other places in New York City."

"I'm meeting with Angelo and Colonel Aldo in an hour. We plan to ask for two or three extra days to do the tourist thing. You and Sofia always look nice. Whatever you pack will be fine, but remember we'll be doing a lot of walking. I'll call when I know how many days we'll be there."

"Okay. Tell Angelo my cousin is worried about the long plane ride."

"Has Sofia been on any long flights?"

"Only short trips. She and Angelo have traveled throughout Europe... nothing like crossing the Atlantic."

"We'll be in business class, everyone will love it."

Nina chuckled. "You're lucky I work for Alitalia. You owe me for the upgrade."

Joe lowered his voice to a whisper. "Take it out in trade."

"Is that all you think about?"

He smiled before he answered. *Why not!* "If you married you, it would also be the prominent thought of your day."

"I'm not complaining. You can make the first installment on your debt when you get home. Don't be late."

"I may be early. I love you."

"Love you too, I'll be waiting."

Nina ended the call, and Joe looked at the framed photo taken at the Target Restaurant the night they met. *Hello, Beautiful. In those red heels you are just the right height.*

Proud of his recent promotion, he lifted the carved wooden nameplate at the front of his desk and turned it. *Chief Inspector Costa. Someone is looking out for me.* After replacing it, he glanced at a document to his left. *Wow. Almost two hundred grand a year. All that, just for ducking bullets, and arresting bad guys.* "I love this job."

Joe slipped into his suit jacket as he left his office. At six foot two, he easily tapped on the top of the door frame at the office next to his. "You ready, Paul?"

DEA Special Agent Paul Sacca, a quiet man more dangerous than he looked, picked up his coat, and they headed down the hall. After Paul spent two successful years' undercover trading drugs for weapons going to the IRA, the Drug Enforcement Administration allowed him to pick his next assignment. He chose Rome hoping he'd be able to reconnect with his family in Verona.

As they neared the elevator, they ran into FBI Special Agent Robert Duffy. *Of all the guys I want to see today, he's the last.* Joe didn't dislike the man. Robert had a good attitude, but took his job, and himself, a little too seriously. *He's a pain in the ass.*

Agent Duffy was the same height as he and Paul but thirty pounds lighter. *Runners aren't built for throwing their weight against immovable objects.*

"You training for next month's marathon?" Paul asked.

"Yeah, why?"

"Looks like you lost a little weight."

Robert shook his head. "No. I gained two pounds this week."

"Fooled the shit out of me," Paul said.

Agent Duffy was like everyone's pesky unwanted little brother. With only four years in the FBI, his assignment to Rome resulted from his important connections. Having an uncle who was the Executive Assistant Director for Science and Technology at FBI Headquarters, had its perks.

"Where you guys headed?" he asked.

"A meeting at Colonel Giuseppe Aldo's office," Joe said.

"Got something going?"

Paul nodded. "DEA's coffee case out of New York."

Joe smiled. *The guy horns in on every investigation he can find.*

Duffy's eyes widened. "I heard about it from the agents handling the racketeering side of the prosecution. Call me if you need any help."

"DEA and the Marshals Service have it covered, but if we get in a bind, and need the Bureau's help, we'll call," Joe said.

Duffy looked at the small box in Joe's hand. "What's in there?"

Joe raised the box. "Coffee... espresso pods."

Duffy lifted his eyebrows. "Is it any good?"

Joe tapped the box. "This shit makes the Colombian and Brazilian Arabica blend taste like pulverized wood."

"I'd love to try it," Duffy said. "Save a few packs for me."

"Expensive stuff," Paul said. "If there's any left we'll bring it to you."

The elevator door opened. Paul and Joe stepped in and waited until it closed before they spoke.

Paul shook his head and shrugged. "He doesn't have a clue."

"He's harmless," Joe said. "I'm surprised a young Italian fashionista hasn't latched onto his ass yet."

"Wouldn't last long."

Joe tilted his head and shot him a quizzical look.

"She'd get bored hearing about the exploits of the FBI. I wouldn't want him anywhere near my sister."

Joe furrowed his brow. "Why not?"

"The Feebs always want to stick their fingers in things."

## Chapter II

### EXPENSIVE COFFEE

Joe, his partner, Carabinieri Captain Angelo Randi, Commander of the Fugitive Task Force, and Paul, waited for the colonel at the polished chestnut wood conference room table. The narrow room was furnished with the table that sat eight, and an Italian flag standing in one corner. It wasn't anything like the colonel's large office, meant to impress or intimidate his visitors.

"After you get back from New York, I won't bother you," Paul said to Angelo. "But I'd appreciate it if you'd keep me informed."

Angelo nodded. "No problem. I'll make sure you get a weekly update. If we get our hands on any of them or something out of the ordinary happens, Joe or I will call."

Angelo stared at the wall and tapped his pen on the table.

"What's wrong?" Joe asked.

"I can be a hard ass. As soon as I open my mouth, the Neapolitans will hear my Roman accent. They won't trust me. You, on the other hand, will get away with murder down there. We may need your Southern Italian charm to get people to talk."

Joe grinned. "So, you're promoting me?"

"Yeah, from partner to close partner and mouthpiece, but don't expect a pay raise."

The door opened and Colonel Giuseppe Aldo entered the conference room. Everyone stood. He motioned for the three men to take their seats and sat in the chair at the head of the table.

Joe gazed at the stubble on his face and his bald head. *Needs to shave twice a day but not one hair on his head.* He caught the colonel's eye and rubbed the side of his cheek. "Looks like you started early today, sir."

Aldo grinned. "One AM. The Carabinieri never sleep." He pointed at the box in front of Joe. "Is that what we've been waiting to get from New York?"

"Yes, sir." He removed one of the tiny espresso pod packages. From his pocket he pulled the switchblade and pressed the lever. "Shall I?"

Aldo nodded.

Joe ripped open the packet and dropped the circular pod onto a piece of paper on the table. He slit open the filter paper and raised a small mound of white powder on the tip of the knife blade. "One packet, seven grams of cocaine, sold for five hundred and sixty to six hundred dollars on the streets of New York."

Angelo raised his eyebrows. "Leave it to the ingenuity of the Neapolitans to come up with something like this. When the Naples command closed the Camorra coffee manufacturing facility, they arrested ten people. They're still in jail awaiting trial."

Paul leaned forward. "The trial for the drug dealers arrested in New York is scheduled to begin next month. All the defendants are on bond because the judge wouldn't consider their flight risk. He said Italians have close-knit families... must have thought they had relatives in the city. Three of them are now missing. He should have asked where their families lived."

"They came home?" Aldo asked.

"Yes, Sir," Paul said. "Our informant said they returned to Naples." He raised his eyebrows. "The metropolitan area is smaller than Rome but they have almost a million more people. It may be difficult to find them."

Aldo looked at Angelo and smiled. "Think your men can handle it?"

"The Neapolitans don't trust people from outside the region of Campania. If we can get someone to talk, we'll find our fugitives."

"Let's discuss New York. You're making arrangements to go there and meet with the investigators?" Aldo asked.

"Yes, sir. Joe is taking Nina on the trip, and with your permission I'd like to take Sofia. We thought we'd extend our stay two days and visit the 9/11 memorial."

"Of course," Aldo said. "If I had the time, I'd go with you. Who will you be meeting?"

Joe removed a paper from his pocket. "DEA Supervisor Al Sarno, NYPD Inspector Michael Cleary, and Marshals Service Fugitive Squad Inspector Harry Walters."

"If you hadn't told me where you were going, I'd assume you'd be staying here in Europe," Aldo said.

Angelo's brow furrowed, and he looked at his boss. "Why is that?"

"Sarno, Cleary and Walters. Italy, Ireland and England. Although, the last time I was in New York City, it was like taking a trip around the world." Aldo placed his elbows on the table, clamped his hands together, and paused. He pointed at the three men. "Remember, what you hear from the investigators in New York relates to the Mafia, not the Camorra in Naples. Earlier I said the Carabinieri never sleep. The clans of the Camorra never close their eyes. They refer to themselves as 'O Sistema, The System' in Neapolitan. Before you look for anyone down there, we need to have another conversation."

"Yes, sir," Angelo replied.

Aldo looked at Joe. "I don't know if I should let you go with Angelo on this one."

"Sir. Please don't take this the wrong way." Joe took a deep breath. "I didn't take this job to sit on my ass in an office in Rome. Angelo and I are cautious. We rely on each other's instincts before we act. Neither of us will do anything stupid."

"I know that. But I worry about the ramifications if an American gets injured in a raid on Italian soil. The other problem is you may have to shoot someone to protect yourself. Members of both governments would jump onto my desk with both feet. I had people nipping at my ass when you got shot during the trawler case."

Angelo interceded. "Sir, I'll protect him as I would any member of my family. He looks Italian, speaks the language fluently, and wears our tactical uniform on operations. I allowed him to place a U.S. Marshals patch beside our patch. If he is to pass for one of us, we'll remove it."

Aldo shrugged. "Our government has already given him permission to carry his weapon. I've been doing this job for a long time... controversy doesn't bother me. But let me think about it."

When he slid his chair back, the others stood.

"Call me later today, Angelo," Aldo said before leaving the room.

Paul tapped Joe on the shoulder. "I envy you, but don't be surprised if the Ambassador doesn't go along with it when he's asked if it's okay for you to work the operation."

Paul was right. Although his boss in Washington didn't worry, the hierarchy at the embassy would want to cover their asses.

Joe grinned. "Who's going to him to ask permission?"

## *Chapter III*

## *THE CITY*

After a long day of sightseeing, Joe, Nina, Angelo and his wife Sofia, crossed the lobby of the Trump International Hotel and Tower next to Central Park. They entered the well-lit bar and sank into leather chairs.

"What did you think of the statue?" Joe asked.

"I didn't know it was that big," Sofia said. "Before we came, I read about it. Lady Liberty, it's a wonderful name."

"It is," Nina said. "When we looked at the exhibits at Ellis Island, I couldn't believe how many Italians came to this country."

Joe nodded. "I read somewhere that between 1900 and 1930, three million Italians, many from the south, immigrated to America."

A waitress took their drink orders.

"Most of the day tomorrow you girls will be on your own. Joe and I are meeting with police officials," Angelo said.

Sofia looked at Nina and grinned. "We'll go shopping."

"I'm sure Angelo and I will be back before five. Don't get lost."

They finished the drinks and headed to their rooms.

### 

The two men arrived at DEA Headquarters on 10th Avenue at eleven the next morning. They walked into an upper floor conference room overlooking the Hudson River and the Chelsea Piers Sport Complex. One of the three men standing at a panoramic window motioned to them. "Come here, it's a good view of the river."

*These guys are huge, well over six feet.* Joe glanced at Angelo, who at five-eleven, was the shortest in the room.

The man who spoke introduced himself and extended his hand. "I'm DEA Supervisor Al Sarno." He motioned to the two men beside him. "NYPD Inspector Michael Cleary, and Marshals Service Fugitive Squad Inspector Harry Walters."

"Nice to meet you. I'm Chief Inspector Joe Costa." He motioned to Angelo. "This is Carabinieri Captain Angelo Randi." Everyone shook hands and took a seat at a table with a pitcher and glasses in the center, and notepads and pens in front of each chair.

"When did you arrive?" Walters asked.

"The day before yesterday. We took time to see a few sights." Joe replied.

Walters turned to Angelo. "Is this your first visit to New York?"

"Yes. Impressive."

"Did you get the package I sent?" Sarno asked.

Joe picked up on his southern drawl. "Yes. It matches the ones seized in Naples. You're not from New York, are you?"

"Been here ten years." Sarno grinned. "Can't shake New Orleans out of my system."

"You're Italian?" Angelo asked.

"Yeah. My grandparents emigrated from Sicily. There's a large Italian population down there and I stay in close contact with my podnas."

"Podnas?" Joe wrinkled his brow.

Cleary smiled. "It takes time to get use to his colloquial expressions. A podna is a friend."

Angelo shook his head. "English is difficult enough. I'll never figure out the local dialects."

Walters handed Angelo and Joe manila folders. "These are the Marshals Service Wanted Posters with information on the guys that skipped town. After the judge issued UFAP warrants, the Marshals Service asked the Justice Department to request your fugitive task force get involved. Your reputation proceeded you."

Angelo glanced at Joe and furrowed his brow.

"UFAP," Joe said. "Unlawful Flight to Avoid Prosecution."

Both men opened the folders and looked at the first page.

"Santo Esposito, aka The Saint," Joe said.

"His involvement matches his size, small time," Walters said. "He's five-six... short and skinny. Wears all black and could pass for an undersized priest. Family is from Naples."

Angelo and Joe flipped to the second page.

"Dominic Capasso, he's called Heads," Angelo said staring at the paper.

"He's the least dangerous of the three... the money guy, and leader of a small group in the Greenwich Village crew," Cleary said. "Short... another peewee. Also five-six, but heavier than The Saint."

They turned to the last page and Joe's eyes widened. "Who's this giant?"

"Francesco Russo. Six four and three hundred plus pounds," Cleary said. "On the street they call him Poco Tonno."

Angelo leaned forward. "Little Tuna? The Japanese only wish half of them were this size."

"He's the midget in the family," Walters said. "See the bottom of the page? His older brother, Johnny, Grande Tonno, is six seven and a little over four hundred pounds. Francesco is the one you need to watch."

"Why?" Joe asked.

Al Sarno tapped the table. "We didn't know the full extent of his involvement until we cultivated an informant. Little Tuna is the enforcer... weapon of choice is the Walther PPKS, 22 long rifle. Killing isn't his only enjoyment in life."

"What else can we look forward to?" Angelo asked.

"The snitch was at his apartment when Francesco cut up a body in the bathtub," Cleary said. "He told us the creep ordered pizza and opened the door in a blood-stained apron... told the delivery guy he was making sauce."

Angelo raised his shoulders and cringed.

"A real nice guy! Is there a complete file on each of these mopes?" Joe asked.

Angelo looked at him and raised his eyebrows.

"Sorry, Ang. A mope is police slang for an unsavory character. We also use the terms dirt-bag and low-life."

Al nodded. "Before we leave for lunch, I'll get the three files off my desk."

### 

When the meeting ended, at a little past one, a black Chevrolet Suburban took them to Pellegrino's restaurant on Mulberry Street, in Lower Manhattan's Little Italy.

Inside, a young man led the five investigators to a round table in an alcove halfway into the narrow dining area. The table could not be seen from the street.

Michael Cleary, in fluent Italian, told the waiter to bring two bottles of red wine and to make it Cabernet Sauvignon.

"You speak Italian well," Angelo said.

"Half Irish and half Italian. My mother is from Naples. She was a school teacher and met my father when he served a tour of duty there. I grew up a few blocks from here."

A man in a white shirt and tie, trailed by a waiter, walked up to the table and looked at Cleary. "Hi Mike. Glad you could come. Who are your friends?"

"Nice to see you again, Tony." Cleary introduced everyone to Tony LaRocca, the manager of Pellegrino's.

Tony nodded to the group. "May I suggest you start with a fine antipasti... the Prosciutto e Melone. The Linguine alla Sinatra, with half a lobster, shrimp, clams, mussels, pine nuts and mushrooms, is excellent as is the veal and filet mignon."

Everyone agreed to let Cleary order the appetizers. "We'll split two orders of Prosciutto e Melone, and two of Mozzarella Della Casa." He nodded to the others. "It's fresh and smoked buffalo mozzarella, tomatoes, roasted peppers and basil."

While Michael Cleary ordered, Joe noticed a man wearing a well-tailored suit and carrying a fedora walk in to the restaurant as if he owned the place. He headed in their direction. *Confident air about him. He looks important... might be the owner.*

Tony saw the gentleman, nodded, and stepped back to let him pass.

When the guy reached their table, Joe saw him turn his head, getting a good look at the five cops. He continued to a corner table at the back of the restaurant.

Tony motioned the waiter to his side and placed a hand on his shoulder. "Enzo and his assistant will serve you. The wine is on me."

Cleary stood. "Thank you." He leaned to Joe and Angelo. "I'll be back in a few minutes. It's been a while since Tony and I talked." The two men headed to the front of the restaurant.

While they waited for the appetizers Al Sarno and Harry Walters asked Angelo questions about the Carabinieri.

"My wife and I were in Rome two years ago," Sarno said to Angelo. "Your guys on the street didn't smile much. I tried to trade a DEA hat and patch for an exploding grenade pin on one of their hats. They wouldn't even discuss it."

Angelo nodded. "Not all of us are unfriendly. It's the image we project that counts. You asked the wrong guy. That pin is difficult to get, but I'll see if I can steal one for you. Give me your address before we leave."

Cleary returned to the table when the appetizers arrived.

Joe started on the delicious food and watched Enzo talk with the well-dressed man. He leaned forward, "Who's the guy in the back of the room? He took a good look at us when he passed the table."

"Vincenzo Rizzo," Cleary said. "He's the Greenwich Village capo in the Genovese family. They call him Vinny No Words. He's quiet and keeps to himself. When I got to the front of the restaurant with Tony, two of Vinny's men were drinking coffee at an outside table. He's a regular here, nothing out of the ordinary. The chef is from the same town in Sicily."

"Is the chef connected?" Joe asked. He noticed Angelo looking at him and the American investigators.

Cleary shook his head. "No. He's religious... kept his nose clean."

"Not connected, but has a clean nose?" Angelo asked. "I don't understand."

Everyone at the table laughed.

"I'm sorry, Angelo," Cleary said. "American idioms are hard to follow. He's not involved with the Mafia and hasn't been in any trouble. Vincenzo helped him get the job. His cousin went to school with him in Sicily."

The five men finished their meal, and over drinks, discussed law enforcement agencies in Italy. At four thirty they drove Joe and Angelo back to Trump Tower.

# Chapter IV

# TOURIST

The next morning Joe, Nina, Angelo and Sofia got out of the Lincoln Navigator on Vesey Street beside One World Trade Center.

Joe leaned into the passenger's side and spoke to the driver before he closed the door. "I'm glad there are Uber drivers with big cars. We'll call you an hour before we want to be picked up and meet you here."

They walked past the entrance to the one hundred and four story building, passed under many of the four-hundred trees surrounding the memorial pools and approached the north pool of the 9/11 Memorial.

Angelo looked back at the tall silver structure and took Sofia's arm. "You want to go to the top before we leave? The observatory is on the hundredth floor."

Sofia pulled him close and everyone looked to the top of the massive building. "How do we get there?"

"Take the elevator at the entrance we passed," Joe said.

Nina looked at Sofia. "Flying doesn't bother me, but riding to the top of that isn't something I want to do."

Sofia raised her eyebrows and nodded. "The plane ride wasn't as bad as I thought it would be, but the elevator doesn't have Business Class. I'll keep my feet on the ground."

"I don't blame you," Angelo said.

Joe took Nina's hand. "Come on."

They walked to the wall surrounding the pool and stared at the names inscribed into the bronze parapets.

"My God. How many names are inscribed here?" Nina asked.

"On this one," Joe pointed at the south pool, "and that one, there are 2,983 names of the men, women, and children killed in the attacks."

"Is this where the buildings stood?" Angelo asked.

"Yes. It's the exact footprint of the two towers. We'll walk to the other one and then go to the museum."

When they turned away from the pool, Joe spotted a man in a black jacket for the second time. *He's the same guy who passed us in front of the building. It's cool but not cold.* He shrugged, but made a mental note of the guy's black combed-back hair.

### 

As if descending into a gigantic tomb, they took the escalator seventy feet below ground.

Nina turned, wide eyed, to Joe. "Not one person has a smile on their face."

"I can understand why."

They stepped into a cavernous room cut out of the earth. A gigantic graffiti covered pillar stood before a section of the original foundation wall.

Angelo turned to Joe. "How big is this place?"

"The museum covers one hundred and ten thousand square feet." He tilted his head and paused. "That's a little under two times the size of the field at the Olympic stadium in Rome. I've heard people say it they took five hours to see everything." He took Nina's hand. "Let's get started."

They walked toward the sixty-foot high exposed section of the World Trade Center's slurry wall that held back seepage from the Hudson River. Joe's eyes came to rest on a black jacket. *Why the jacket? Maybe he's from down south... Central America.* He stopped, shook his head, and turned away from the man.

"What's wrong?" Angelo asked.

"Don't anyone react to what I say. Act like we are having a normal conversation and please do not turn toward him. Directly behind me, near the wall, there's a man in a black jacket. I've seen him three times since we got out of the car."

"Are we being followed?" Angelo asked.

Joe shrugged. "I'm not sure. Let's walk past the next three exhibits and then stop. We'll see if he stays with us."

"Okay." Angelo stepped in front of Nina and Sofia. "Don't make eye contact with him. If you turn in his direction, focus on something to the side."

They stopped beside a fire truck partially destroyed when the buildings fell.

Joe asked the others to stand beside the truck for a good camera shot. Out of the corner of his eye he noticed the man standing thirty feet behind the exhibit. He moved to the side and raised his Nikon so he could position the stranger in the background of the photo.

"Everyone smile." With the camera pointed at the group he zoomed in on the man's face and took two pictures.

Angelo stepped in close. "Did you get a good picture of him?"

"Yeah, a great shot of his face."

Angelo raised his eyebrows. "What are you thinking?"

"Someone wants to find out more about us." Joe said. "Remember the guy at the restaurant? He's the key to this. People on Mulberry Street in Little Italy need to live with the wiseguys. When they go into a restaurant and ask questions, they expect an answer. I'm sure by now they know we're here, but they may not know why."

"And if they do?"

Joe shrugged. "They might pass the word to friends back in Italy."

Angelo pondered and rubbed his chin. "The Saint and his friends aren't stupid. They realize we'll be looking for them."

"True, but one thing bothers me."

"What?"

"Are they going to be told who's doing the looking?"

## *Chapter V*

## *WISEGUYS*

The waiter at Nougatine, inside the Trump International Hotel, set the after-dinner drinks on the table. "Are you sure you don't want dessert?"

Joe glanced at Angelo and the women. They all shook their heads. "No thank you, we're fine. Everything was excellent."

He handed Joe the bill. "Thank you for coming to Nougatine," and walked away.

"What time does the plane leave tomorrow?" Sofia asked Nina.

"At four-twenty. We'll fly all night and land before seven the next morning. Want to get up early and go to Times Square?"

Sofia looked at Joe. "Do we have time?"

"Sure. We need to leave for the airport by twelve-fifteen. Michael Cleary from the New York City police department will meet us in front of the Alitalia counter at two." He slid cash into the bill folio and they left the restaurant.

### 

That evening two men in suits walked into the lobby of the hotel and stopped at the reception desk. Ralph, the taller man, motioned to the desk clerk, while his partner turned and observed the lobby.

"Excuse me." He pointed at the clerk's nametag. "Stephen. How ya doing?"

"Fine, sir. How may I help you?"

"Earlier today, my boss noticed two Italian guys in the lobby. He thinks he may have met one of them in Rome." Ralph handed him a photo of Joe and Angelo. "Could you give me their names?"

Stephen bit his lip. "I'm sorry, sir. For security reasons we may not give out that information without the guest's permission."

Ralph opened his hand, unfolded a pair of hundred-dollar bills, and slid them toward the clerk. "I understand,

Stephen, but my boss is a powerful man, and he doesn't like hearing the word no. Maybe you should make an exception for him."

The clerk glanced to an office door at the end of the counter. "I don't want to lose my job, sir. Sorry, I can't help you."

"That's too bad." Ralph motioned toward the lobby. "Mr. Trump must be a wonderful employer and pay you well. Does he offer hospitalization insurance? Something to pay the bill should you have an accident on the job? Ya know, like one or two broken legs." He slid the bills closer to the clerk.

Stephen took the money. "One moment, please." He shuffled through a card file, scribbled on a piece of paper and pushed it across the counter.

Ralph lifted the paper. "Angelo Randi and Joseph Costa. Yes, I believe he knows Mr. Randi." He shoved the paper into his pocket. "Thank you, Stephen. My boss and I wish you good health." Ralph pointed to Stephen's wedding band. "Also your wife, and kids, if you have any." Both men and left without looking back.

###

Vincenzo Rizzo held a Coke glass half-filled with red wine. He sat on a couch in the back room of a bar in Greenwich Village. On an end table next to him lay a plate piled high with a variety of savory cheeses. He seldom missed a Rangers game and stared at the television on the wall.

Ralph stepped into the room. "Hi, Vinny. I got the names you wanted." He handed his boss the paper.

"Good." Vinny scanned the note. "Over at Pellegrino's, Enzo said one of them was a Carabinieri Captain... powerful man. Ya don't wanna fuck with him. The other *chooch* is a U.S. Marshal. One of those *mamalukes* who hide the snitches."

Ralph scrunched his eyebrows. "Hide snitches?"

"Yeah. Remember, Sammy the Bull, and Joe Dogs Iannuzzi, the cook? Them guys... the snitches."

Ralph's eyes widened. "The G's protection program for rats?"

"Yeah. I'll call Dante in Naples tonight. He'll wanna know they're here asking questions."

## Chapter VI

## THE BLUEPRINT

A week after he and Angelo returned to Rome, Joe sat in on a meeting at Colonel Aldo's conference room.

In attendance were the colonel, Angelo, DEA Special Agent Paul Sacca, Sacca's counterpart Lieutenant Sergio Lacona of the Carabinieri Counter-Narcotics Group, and FBI Special Agent Robert Duffy.

After the group spent thirty minutes discussing the case, Aldo glanced at the five men. "Are there questions about Angelo's report of the New York trip?"

They all shook their heads.

"Coordinating the investigation could become a problem," Aldo said. "I spoke with the colonel at the Counter Narcotics Group. Lieutenant Lacona and his men will monitor the case here in Rome. The Fugitive Task Force will take the lead and attempt to make the arrest in or around

Naples." Aldo motioned to Duffy. "Agent Duffy, this is your first case with us. Again, I want to welcome you to our group."

"Thank you, sir. I'm looking forward to providing you with the FBI's help."

"We welcome all the help we can get, but for now you and Agent Sacca will stay in Rome. Sergio assures me you'll both get access to the Counter Narcotics Group."

Duffy took a deep breath. "But, sir. The FBI has the ability..."

The colonel interrupted him. "There are no butts in my office Agent Duffy. We are flexible, and will use all the resources of the FBI and DEA should my Fugitive Task Force need them. Until that time, Captain Randi, Inspector Costa, and their men will work the case in Naples."

"Yes, sir," Duffy replied.

"Good. I don't want any of the problems that arise when different agencies compete against each other. Questions anyone?"

The men remained silent.

"Thank you, gentlemen. I need to speak with Angelo and Joe."

Sergio, Paul and Duffy left the room.

When the door closed, Colonel Aldo continued. "Back to what we discussed before your New York trip." He looked at Angelo. "I will allow Joe to work the case with you. I told Agent Duffy there were no butts in my office, but I have a few instructions you are to follow."

"Thank you, sir," Joe said. "We'll abide by any rules you set."

"Both of you listen. I want to make sure nothing happens during this operation that will embarrass us. Joe's not to dress any different than you and your men... nothing that could identify him as an American."

Angelo smiled. "A week ago he picked up new Carabinieri tactical uniforms to include boots. The bullet-proof vest he brought from America is in his office and I gave him one of ours."

Aldo turned to Joe. "Put your Glock with your American vest. Angelo, issue him one of our Beretta pistols. Take submachine guns. I seem to recall you and your men received the new H&K MP5?"

"Yes, sir."

Aldo raised his eyebrows. "Don't ask for another one to give to Joe. Tomorrow I'll bring in the one I keep at my house."

*Wow. He's putting his ass on the line.* Joe leaned over the table. "Sir, you don't have to do that."

"I know." Aldo stared at him. "I wouldn't if I didn't trust you. Remember you are not dealing with structured Mafia families that have a defined chain of command. The Camorra is composed of formless and autonomous clans. Honor plays no part. Control is imposed by force... often violent. The members do not worry about their next birthday celebration. You both need to learn more about them before you start your operation. Now, tell me what you and Joe plan to do."

"We're going to Naples for a few days to get familiar with the surroundings. During that time, we'll formalize a plan. When we return, we'll brief you and the others and then go back with a team from the Task Force."

Aldo nodded and stood. "Be careful." He looked at Joe. "Do you know the motto of your Special Forces?"

"Yes, sir. *De Oppresso Liber*, to liberate the oppressed."

Aldo grinned. "Forget it. The oppressed don't want to be liberated. Best if you follow the motto of the Special Air Service, *Who Dares Wins*."

## *Chapter VII*

## *THE ADVANCE*

Angelo and his wife Sofia arrived at Joe and Nina's apartment at eight that evening. They spent the next three hours sitting around the dining room table talking, drinking and eating the appetizers Nina prepared.

The conversation remained light. Neither man wanted to alarm the women with details of their planned trip, but both wives knew they were leaving in the next few days.

Joe glanced at Angelo. *Got to tease him a little.* "When we get back are you going to invite Nina and me to San Lorenzo so we can visit with your neighbor, the Pope?" Joe asked.

Sofia raised her eyebrows. "You've never been to Castel Gandolfo?"

"I have, but Joe hasn't," Nina said.

Angelo laughed. "Sure, we'll have you come to dinner. The Pope's residence is nearby but I hope you aren't expecting a personal invitation from His Holiness?"

Joe looked at him and smiled. *Come on, Angelo.* "Why not? You have connections with the Swiss Guard. I'll bet the Pope never met a U.S. Marshal."

"I have friends in high places," Angelo said, "but few of them are that close to heaven." His phone rang. "Excuse me." He walked away from the table.

A minute of casual conversation passed and Angelo called Joe's name.

He walked into the living room. "What is it?"

"One of our men believes he saw The Saint in Naples."

"A guy on our Task Force?"

"Yes." He tilted his head toward the dining room. "We need to tell them we're leaving tomorrow."

### 

Early the next afternoon Joe and Angelo pulled into the driveway of a safe house twenty miles outside Naples. Angelo stopped the car and waited for the automatic gate to retract allowing access to the property. He then drove a hundred feet to a villa on an oversized lot.

Upon entering the house, Joe saw Claudio, one of the Task Force officers involved in the shooting in Rome. "Hi Claudio. Haven't seen you in six months."

"The day you stopped a bullet with your arm," Claudio said. "Have you had any problems with it?"

Joe raised his left hand and flexed his fist. "No. Everything still works, but it left me with a hell of a scar."

Angelo introduced him to two other Task Force officers. Gennaro appeared to be a short teenager, but shook Joe's hand with the grip of a flyweight wrestler. Sabatino was the largest of the three. The muscular six-foot tall man had hands larger than Joe had ever seen. The first two knuckles bore thick calluses.

Angelo led everyone to a room with a large table and eight chairs. A white dry-erase board hung on one wall. A table with a laptop and two projectors stood in the corner.

Once everyone took a seat, Angelo broke the silence. "What do you have planned for us in the morning, Claudio?"

"Two days ago, in the town of Sant'Antonio Abate, thirty minutes from here, Gennaro and I saw a man that fits Santo Esposito's description."

"Where?" Joe asked.

"We've been watching a market, a bar, and a few more locations frequented by the clan. He came out of a local market one block from a bar that's known as a clan hangout. The place is called Caesar's Bar. It appears to be a typical local business... coffee, liquor, pastry, small meals, and gelato. We didn't go there. They would have known we're from out of town."

Angelo spent a moment staring at the table and then looked at Claudio. "Are you sure it was him?"

"No. Later I'll set up the computer and projector and show you the photos we took."

"Did Santo go into the bar?" Joe asked.

"No. He stopped outside and said something to a man coming out the door. They spoke for five minutes, then he turned down an alley and we couldn't follow him without being seen."

"Okay," Angelo said. "When we're done here, I want to take a drive past that bar."

### 

Two hours later Angelo turned his gray Alfa Romeo onto a narrow street in Sant'Antonio Abate. Joe sat in the front and Claudio in the back.

Joe glanced to the back seat. "How far is it from here?"

"One kilometer. It will be on the left."

Joe studied the road in front of the car. *Not very wide.* "Is this street always crowded with cars, Claudio?"

"Yes, but late at night there's not much traffic. Cars may park on the right side. You'll seldom find a vacant space."

An empty feeling developed in Joe's stomach. The driver's side mirrors on the parked cars were folded in to allow passing vehicles a few more inches. "Glad you're not driving a big Ford or Chevy, Ang. This Alfa barely squeezes through here."

Angelo laughed. "The road has been here longer than America has been a country."

Joe looked at the two and three-story buildings lining the street. The three-foot-wide sidewalks in front of the structures provided little room for people to stop and talk while others passed. Many of the people talking stood in the small space between the parked cars. It would tempt fate to step off the sidewalk on the left side of the street.

"How much farther?" Angelo asked.

"A hundred meters," Claudio replied.

Joe scanned the buildings ahead.

"Up there, on the left. The sign is above the door." Claudio said.

Angelo slowed as they passed the entrance to the bar. Two men, leaning against the wall near the doorway, looked at the Alfa Romeo as it passed. Joe glanced over his shoulder and noticed one of them pointing at the car.

Fifty feet past the bar, a bullet shattered the back window and tore into the center console.

Claudio threw himself down on the seat and Joe ducked as Angelo hit the gas.

### 

Later that night Joe sat with Gennaro and Sabatino in the makeshift conference room at the safe house. No one spoke. Gennaro shuffled through a stack of papers and Sabatino cleaned his fingernails with a pocket knife.

Joe stared at the wall and took a deep breath. *We haven't started yet and already someone takes a shot at us. The colonel was right. These bastards are dangerous. We need more firepower than handguns.*

Angelo and Claudio walked in and sat at the table. Angelo turned to Gennaro and Sabatino. "Did Claudio and Joe tell you about our back window?"

Both men nodded, their eyes locked on their boss.

Angelo tapped the table with his fingers. "This will not go unanswered." He looked at Claudio. "Get two more men and two of our marked Land Rovers. I want these bastards to know they are dealing with the Carabinieri. We'll raid the bar at ten tonight."

Sabatino raised a finger. "How did they figure out it was you in the car?"

"I don't think they did," Angelo said. "The car attracted their attention. It may be unmarked, but an Alfa Romeo with three men in it, and two of them in suits, was something they've seen many times. Carabinieri may not be written on the side, but, when they looked at it, that's what they saw."

*Someone is protecting the place,* Joe thought. "The round didn't come from street level. It had to be fired from a rooftop to end up in the console."

"Joe's right," Angelo said. "The five of us will take the bar, have the other two in street clothes and tell them to get to the top of the highest nearby building."

"Tactical gear?" Gennaro asked.

Angelo nodded. "Vests, masks, and I want each of us to carry a MP5."

Joe smiled. *What's that old saying? God protects children and fools. The MP5 will even out the odds.*

## Chapter VIII

## CAESAR'S BAR

At 9:30 that night, Joe watched Angelo glance into the rearview mirror at the police car behind their Land Rover. Blue flashing lights lit the dark street.

"This is a good spot. Even though we have one of our men with the local officer, I don't want them getting any closer," Angelo said. He stopped, stuck his hand out the window and pointed at the ground.

The sedan turned and blocked the street. The officer and Carabiniere got out.

"They won't let any cars pass until we tell them. We'll wait until the street clears and Claudio calls," Angelo said.

Joe pointed the barrel of his MP5 at the floorboard and placed the weapon between his legs. He set his balaclava face mask on his thigh and tightened one strap of his protective vest. *Hope this goes well. Never seen Angelo this angry.* The bullet that shattered the rear window of Angelo's car wasn't meant to hit anyone. Someone wanted to intimidate them. *This will be interesting. Ang will kick ass.*

"Say nothing in English while we're there."

"I won't." Joe smiled. "I'll try to keep my mouth shut, look mean and make sure everyone is safe." He glanced to the back seat. "You ready, Gennaro?"

"Yes, sir."

The radio crackled and Claudio's voice blared from the speaker. "Moving now."

Angelo pulled the mask over his head and put the Land Rover in gear.

### 

Claudio's SUV came from the opposite direction and skidded to a stop in front of the bar. He and Sabatino, with two other Carabinieri leapt out seconds before Joe and Angelo came to a stop.

Two men standing on the sidewalk dashed into an alley. A young man bolted out of the bar and Sabatino stuck out his arm. His rigid forearm slammed into the man's jaw.

Joe's mouth fell open, and he froze. Everything seemed to move in slow motion. He cringed as the guy's head stopped when it met Sabatino's muscular forearm. *Holy shit!* The man's feet continued to race from the scene. Both of his legs left the ground, and for a split second his prone body hung three feet above the concrete. The man dropped and moaned when his back and head hit the sidewalk. *That hurt!*

Sabatino dragged the body from the entrance, placed a boot on the unconscious man's chest, and smiled.

Joe and Angelo jumped from their vehicle.

"Stay behind me!" Angelo yelled.

They left an officer to secure the vehicles and cover the alley.

Sabatino and Gennaro followed Angelo and Joe into the bar.

Angelo looked at Joe and pointed to a frail, gray-haired woman sitting at a corner table. "Watch her." With Sabatino and Gennaro leading, he headed to a back room.

Joe lowered his weapon, moved away from the door, and glanced around the stale smelling room. Dusty tables and two near-empty pastry and gelato cases caught his eye. One tub of ice cream and two small trays of broken cookies were the only items on display in the cabinets. Four shelves behind the bar held only three bottles of whiskey. *This bar isn't selling anything.* He focused on the old woman. "From the looks of this place, there's not much business."

The woman shrugged. "You're from Naples."

"No. Milan. All of us are dressed for the late night opera at the La Scala Theater."

She laughed. "If you wanted me to believe that, you should have written it on paper. The sounds of Naples came out of your mouth."

Angelo returned. "A meeting room. Two slot machines, card tables and a big television. Everyone in there ran out the back door." He walked to the woman. "Where is the owner?"

"You're speaking to her. The bar closed last year."

"Where do you live?"

She hesitated. "In the apartment upstairs."

"Why do you have slot machines?" Angelo asked.

"Entertainment. They pay no money, only a paper with a score. My friends come here to enjoy the soccer games on a large television."

"Your friends weren't interested in the rest of the game. They left their drinks on the table when they ran."

The woman raised her palms in front of her and shrugged.

Sabatino came out of the room. "They're gone. The street out back and the alley are clear."

"You and your men wait here until the local police arrive," Angelo said. "Don't allow anyone to touch the box of receipts and credit cards near the slot machines." He turned to the woman. "Stay in that chair, the Financial Police will want to speak to you when they arrive."

The woman leaned forward and spat.

Angelo took a step back and glared at her. "Signora," he said in a sarcastic tone. "Was it your mother who taught you to spit on the floor?"

He headed to the door, paused and turned to Sabatino. "Please call the local health service. Ask them to inspect this woman's apartment to make sure it's livable. She has the bad habit of discharging body fluids on the floor."

The woman stood and stared at him with a contorted expression that turned to a smile. "You have beautiful eyes, Carabiniere."

Angelo glared at her. "Be careful, old woman. Imagine what will happen if I tell your neighbors and friends we had a long friendly conversation about their activities."

Joe followed him out the door.

### 

During their drive to the safe house, Joe kept quiet. *Ang is pissed!* After ten minutes, Angelo's hands relaxed on the steering wheel. *He'll talk now.*

"Did you hear what she said, Ang?"

"Yes."

"You know that wasn't a compliment she gave you." Joe said.

"I know. It isn't the first time it's happened. As soon as she spoke I knew what she meant. It was a curse... the evil eye." Angelo looked at him, faked a shiver and grinned. "I'm worried."

Joe shook his head. "When people down here do that, I get nervous."

Angelo couldn't hide his smile. "Do you have a horn for protection?"

"Yes, on a chain. It's in a drawer in my bedroom."

Angelo raised his eyebrows. "Can I borrow it when we go home?"

"Hell no, Ang. Buy your own. I'm putting it on as soon as we get to Rome. What are you thinking?"

"The one thing they respect is force. I want them to see the power of the Carabinieri Fugitive Squad. Tomorrow we'll go back to Rome. You get your horn, and then we'll brief the colonel."

# Chapter IX

# NO MEN OF HONOR

Colonel Aldo motioned Angelo and Joe into his office. He pointed to the leather couch in front of the coffee table and they took a seat. Angelo set a thick folder between them.

Joe leaned forward and rubbed his hand across the table. *Black marble with veins of gold... beautiful.*

Aldo sat in an armchair across from them. "How long have you been back?" Aldo asked Angelo.

"Three days."

The colonel pointed at Joe. "Do you still want to help Angelo on this case?"

"Yes, sir. The Camorra may be dangerous, but they're too smart to do something as dumb as shooting an officer. One bullet through the back window of our car was their attempt to frighten us."

"I agree, Inspector Costa, but be careful. You and Angelo are working a case against organized crime, but like I said, it's not the Mafia you face."

Joe scratched his cheek and squinted. "What do you mean, sir?"

"The Mafia thinks of themselves as honorable men. Have you heard that term?"

"Yes, sir."

"Their criminal organization accepts only full-blooded Italians as members... most from Sicily. Their men spend years working and waiting to become members of the family. They are loyal to a 'Don', the head of the family."

"I understand that, sir," Joe said. "But the Camorra, in its own way, has the same structure."

"That is where you are mistaken. The Camorra draws its members from the streets. Have you read anything by Isa Sales?" Aldo asked.

"No, sir."

"He's an expert on Italian organized crime. He said, 'Camorra soldiers come from the lowest socio-economic echelons, the urban sub-proletariat.' Unlike the Mafia, anyone can join a Camorra gang. Sales described the Clans as having no central organization. Their loyalty is to crime and money."

"Isn't that the same as the Mafia?" Joe asked.

Aldo shook his head. "No. When we go after the men, or the head of a Mafia family, they don't take it personal. They may threaten law enforcement officials, but they seldom act on the threats."

"What about Giovanni Falcone, the judge and prosecuting magistrate? The Mafia killed him with a bomb in 1992," Angelo said.

Aldo nodded. "Yes, in Sicily. A half-ton of explosives in a culvert under the road. By early 1993 the boss responsible for the murder, Salvatore Riina, they call him The Beast, paid for it. We arrested him and brought his family to their knees."

"I remember the case," Angelo said.

Joe looked at Colonel Aldo and tilted his head.

"You don't know about Falcone's death?" Aldo asked.

Joe shook his head. "No, sir."

"Angelo, tell him about it later. The government went after Riina's organization. The Mafia learned a lesson, but the Clans in Naples didn't pay attention. Men of the

Camorra, from the war-torn countries of the Middle East and Africa, don't value life as we do. Many of them have sworn allegiance to terrorist groups. They don't care who they kill."

"The difference is interesting," Joe said, "but I still want to help the Fugitive Squad. I helped create it."

Angelo shifted his position on the couch. "Sir. Has anyone brought up the shooting in the trawler case?"

"Not for a while. The politicians worried after Joe got shot in the arm. When I spoke to the Director of the Marshals Service, he told me Joe is safer here than on the streets of Chicago or New York City." Aldo paused, rubbed the stubble on his chin, and stared at both men. "Both of you be careful. Now, what's your next move?"

"Three of my men remained at the safe house. We'll brief the other twelve men I'm taking." Angelo said. "I'll contact Naples Carabinieri Command, and if more men are needed, I'll speak with the State and Municipal police."

Aldo waved a hand. "No. I want you to be more cautious. I'll arrange for you to meet with Colonel Ferrara. Brief him, and no one else. Contact no other police until the moment you need their help. The local officers live and have families in those communities. One passing comment about Carabinieri from Rome looking for three fugitives could be disastrous."

"Angelo and I will put six men in plain clothes on the street. Does Colonel Ferrara need to be told?"

"Yes, but I'll make the call. All raids are to be conducted in tactical uniforms. I don't want one Clan to think another started a war. Anything else to discuss?"

Angelo tapped the folder next to his leg. "Yes, sir. We received information from DEA in New York. They provided us with family addresses of the three fugitives. The men working undercover will check out each location."

"Anything more?" Aldo asked.

"No, sir."

"We're leaving the day after tomorrow," Joe said.

"Watch out for that big guy," warned Aldo.

Joe grinned. "Francesco... Little Tuna?"

Aldo raised his eyebrows, "Yeah. Little lard-ass tuna."

## Chapter X

## CAMORRA EYES

That night Joe and Nina finished dinner in their apartment. After clearing the dishes, they relaxed, sipping cold yellow Limoncello liqueur from shot glasses. He looked across the table at his wife. *I never get tired of looking at her, she's so beautiful. I'm a lucky man.*

"Angelo and I are going to Naples in two days, and we'll be there about a week."

Nina tapped her fingers on the table and frowned. "Not another trip out of town. Are you trying to find more fugitives?" She took a sip of her drink.

"Yeah. The three from New York. Remember the case I told you about while we were there?"

Nina shook her head. "I thought you would have found them by now."

"I wish it was that easy," Joe sighed. "What's your flight schedule?"

"The day after tomorrow I fly to Miami for one night. The return flight comes into Milan and I transfer planes to get back to Rome. After that I have three days of flights to different places in Europe. If you're not back by then, I'll call Sofia and we'll go shopping."

Joe smiled. "So, we'll be out of town at the same time. Miami returns to Miami."

"Don't bring up the Omar Hassan case. I'm still mad at you and Angelo for giving me that name."

"It worked." Joe chuckled. "Thank God they didn't find out your real name." He tapped his glass against hers. "I'll always love Miami."

Nina stuck her tongue out at him and then downed the last drops of her Limoncello.

### 

Neither Bruno, nor his cousin Josef, thought much about the Camorra. They didn't sell drugs or engage in any activities they considered criminal. Helping The Scorpion keep members of his gang in line was nothing more to the cousins than a well-paying job. The police did little when they found a drug dealer with two broken legs or a thief beaten half to death in an alley. Bruno could not recall the Carabinieri ever taking time to investigate the murder of a Camorra soldier. *We're doing them a favor.*

Bruno pulled onto a narrow street in the Campo Marzio section of central Rome. He slowed the old Fiat in front of the apartment building and noticed a vacant parking space. *Amazing... a place to park at night in Rome. This place is worse than Naples.* He pulled into the spot and turned off the engine. *Let's not attract attention.* He pointed to the door of a building across the street. "That's the entrance. The apartment is on the second floor."

"The American, Costa?"

"Yeah."

Josef nodded. "What's his wife's name?"

"Nina Belsogno. She's Italian. They married here in Rome."

"What about the other one?"

"Angelo Randi. Nico said he's a corrupt Carabinieri captain. His wife Sofia is also a Belsogno... the wives are cousins. Nico doesn't want us to tell anyone we know about them. One of D'Arco's men told him about a telephone call from a Mafioso in America." He started the engine.

"Okay," Josef said. "Where does the captain live?"

"In San Lorenzo, not far from Castel Gandolfo. We'll drive there now."

"An apartment building?"

"No. A villa. Carabinieri captains are well paid."

### 

The next morning, sixty-year-old clan leader, Dante D'Arco sat at his desk in a cramped bedroom he had converted into a home office. The old wooden desk wasn't large but served its purpose. *I'm the boss.* The faint sound of opera came from a stereo on a bookcase against a wall.

Nico Basso, the leader of his largest gang, slouched in one of two chairs in front of the desk. Dante didn't like the man. He tolerated him, but head strong Nico seldom thought before he acted.

Dante stared at a black and green tattoo of a scorpion on the young man's neck. The pincers and fearsome tail clearly visible, and ready to strike. *Why would anyone want a bug on his skin?* "You said you'd have that tattoo covered."

"The scorpion? It's my mark and the reason everyone fears me. I don't know anyone who isn't afraid of them. The three Americans even keep their distance."

"They are not Americans, Nico." Dante glared at him. "Our friends once lived in New York but they are Italians, and their families work for me."

Nico took a deep breath and nodded. "Sorry. Santo will be here in a few minutes. They're lucky they weren't at the bar when the Carabinieri went there."

"Tell everyone to stay away from the old woman's place. The neighbors have been talking. It seems she spent a long time with the officers."

Santo walked into the room and Dante pointed at a chair.

He sat, shot a questioning look at Nico, and turned back to Dante. "Good morning Mr. D'Arco."

"Good morning, Santo. Are your friends safe?"

"Yes. We are staying at Francesco's brother-in-law Gino's house."

Dante waved a hand toward Nico. "Thank you for arranging this meeting. I'll have someone drive Santo back to the house."

As Nico left the room, Santo's eyes lingered on the doorway.

"Is something wrong?" Dante asked.

"No. I'm uncomfortable around him."

"Many people are," Dante said. "Tell the others to stay away from him and his men. One of them shot the window out of an Alfa Romeo near Caesar's Bar. The dumb bastard said it looked like something the Carabinieri would drive and he wanted to screw with them."

"I'll bet it scared the shit out everyone in the car. Did you get any news from New York?"

"Yes. Vincenzo Rizzo called me. Two police officers from Italy met with New York cops. We're sure it was about you and your friends. He thought they were both Italian, but one is an American who works at the embassy in Rome. His name is Joseph Costa, and he's helping a Carabinieri captain named Angelo Randi."

"Are they the same ones who raided the bar?"

"I don't know. We have photos from across the street but they all wore masks."

Santo sighed. "Should we leave town?"

"No. You're safe here. My men are watching for any Carabinieri vehicles." He stood and Santo left.

## Chapter XI

# LITTLE TUNA

Few people would guess Francesco Russo had the street name Little Tuna. It made no sense for a man who stood six foot four and topped three hundred pounds. He and The Saint sat at the kitchen table in his sister Maria's house.

She stood in front of-the stove preparing pasta and asparagus in a frying pan. The smell of cooked garlic and tomato sauce permeated the room. Chicken breasts and mushrooms sizzled in a pan on the back burner.

Santo scooped two slices of prosciutto, capicola, soppressata, and a ball of buffalo mozzarella onto his plate. Franco filled their glasses with red wine, emptied the plate of sliced meat and took two balls of the soft white cheese. He passed a basket of sliced homemade bread to Santo.

"Will the old man continue to help us?" Francesco asked as he stuffed prosciutto into his mouth.

"Yeah, but he wants us to stay away from The Scorpion and his crew."

*Asshole,* Francesco thought as he took a bite of bread, and spoke with a full mouth. "That scorpion meatball wouldn't last a week with Vinny and our crew back home. If he tries to break my balls, I'll crush him like a bug."

"The guy's a nut case. Better if we avoid him."

Franco nodded. "What's the skinny with the American cop? NYPD?"

Maria placed a bowl of pasta in front each man.

Francesco put his hands together as if praying and raised and lowered them. "Jeeze, this all I get?" He stared at the plate piled high with macaroni.

Maria smacked him in the back of the head. "Christ, Franco, finish that first. I'm making enough chicken to feed the priest and his altar boys, then you'll get salad."

"Thank you, Maria," Santo said.

She rolled her eyes and returned to the stove.

"The American cop." Francesco prompted.

"Oh, yeah. He works at the U. S. Embassy... must be a feeb. No way will they find us here."

"Good. When we're done eating, let's go for pizza."

### 

Gennaro, wearing civilian clothes instead of his usual uniform, had spent the last four hours in and out of shops on a side street closed to vehicles. He was one of four men Claudio had assigned to various parts of town, hoping one of them would see the fugitives. *It's getting crowded.* His stomach growled at the instant he spotted an inviting sign. *Pizzeria Mezza Luna... perfect.*

He walked into the restaurant, stepped to the counter, and nodded to the man in a dough and tomato stained white shirt. Four precooked pizzas lay on a slab of marble behind a glass partition. "I'll take a large slice of the Margherita."

"Something to drink?" the man asked.

"No, and I'll take the pizza with me."

The man cut a generous slice, wrapped it in butcher paper and handed it to him. "Two Euros."

He dropped the money on the counter, stepped back, and bounced off the man behind him. Gennaro, turned. His eyes focused on the black button of a massive tan shirt. *A friggin giant.* He raised his head, his heart fluttered, and he quit breathing. *Holy shit. Little Tuna!*

"You done, little man?" the giant said.

Gennaro rocked from side to side and glanced at the man standing next to the big guy. *Black pants, black shirt, black sports coat. It's The Saint!*

Santo motioned with his thumb to the man behind him. "Dance with Gino. Move so we can get something to eat today, not tomorrow."

"Sorry." *Damn! Three of them, get out now.* He hurried out of the restaurant. Ten feet past the door, he stopped, leaned against the building, unwrapped the pizza and took a bite. *Should I follow them?*

### 

That afternoon, Joe nodded to Angelo, Claudio and Gennaro as he entered the living room at the safe house and took a seat. He smiled at Gennaro. *I've got to ask him.* "Is he that big?"

"Jesus, sir. You ever hear the ancient Greek story about the mythological giant Mimos?"

"Sure. He's buried under Mount Vesuvius."

"Well, the bastard escaped. And when I saw him at that pizzeria, he looked hungry."

"Anything else?" Angelo asked.

Gennaro shook his head. "No. I wish I could have followed them, but they got a good look at me. If they had seen me after I walked out the door, they would have been suspicious."

"And you're sure the three of them were together?"

"Yes. The Saint didn't hesitate when he pointed at the third guy."

"Gino? Right?" Angelo asked.

"Yes."

Angelo lifted three file folders from the coffee table. He set two aside, opened the third and scanned the pages. "Is this the guy?" He handed Gennaro a police mug-shot.

"Yeah."

"Gino Di Napoli," Angelo said. "Little Tuna's brother-in-law. He married the fat guy's sister, Maria." Angelo flipped through two pages and stopped. "He works on the docks in Naples."

"Is it close to where they made the coffee pods?" Joe asked.

"Yes. Three blocks away."

Angelo turned to Gennaro. "And you didn't see Dominic Capasso?"

"No, the place was crowded. He could have been sitting at a table."

Angelo handed the folder to Claudio. "The sister's address is in here. Make sure the family still lives there. If they do, assign two men to take pictures of the house. Call headquarters in Rome and find out if we have any recent aerial photos of the house and the surrounding area."

"Think they would be dumb enough to stay with family members?" Joe asked.

Angelo smiled. "They left Italy twelve years ago. I'm betting they see Naples as it was back then and don't realize the Carabinieri uses the latest technology like the rest of the world."

"You thinking about raiding the place?" Joe asked.

Angelo nodded and grinned. "If we can verify they are staying there. If not, we'll be nice and knock on the front door."

## *Chapter XII*

## *COMMANDO NAPOLI*

The next morning, Joe smiled as a junior officer led him and Angelo to Colonel Ferrara's office at Carabinieri Command in Naples. Angelo wore his uniform, and he wore a dark gray suit. Joe allowed Angelo to do all the talking since they arrived. *No one knows I'm American.*

In a wide hallway with framed photos of retired officers lining the walls, the young man pointed to a doorway and stepped aside.

Joe and Angelo walked into the colonel's outer office and stopped in front of the secretary's desk. "I'm Captain Randi." He motioned to Joe. "Chief Inspector Costa, we're from Rome."

Joe smiled at the slim well figured woman in a tight white dress. *Early to mid-thirties.*

"Welcome to Naples. Colonel Ferrara is waiting for you." She led them to a door and opened it.

Colonel Mauro Ferrara met them in the center of the office and shook their hands. "Come in, Angelo." Mauro pointed to a round table with four chairs in the corner of the office and looked at Joe. "And you must be U.S. Marshal Chief Inspector Costa."

"Yes, sir. Please call me Joe."

Mauro wasn't a tall man, but he was stocky and had streaks of gray peppered through his wavy black hair and goatee. Joe scanned the office. *Not as elegant as Colonel Aldo's, but nice.* A large carved wooden insignia of the Special Intervention Group hung on the wall behind the colonel's executive desk. He noticed the paratrooper badge above Mauro's breast pocket.

Everyone sat, and the colonel looked at Joe. "Welcome to our command. Few visitors from American law enforcement come here."

*Colonel Aldo must have told him.* "Thank you, sir. It's a pleasure to meet you."

"It's my pleasure to meet someone from near my home."

"Boston?" Joe asked.

"No. Your family in Italy... the Province of Salerno."

Joe's eyes widened. "I thought I recognized the accent. Where do they live?"

"Vietri Sul Mare, not far from the port. The Ferrara family owns the largest ceramic shop in town."

Joe smiled. "A beautiful little town. The Amalfi Coast is one of my favorite places in Italy."

Mauro turned to Angelo. "Your boss and I had a long conversation. He told me about the case. You're looking for three men who fled to Naples following their arrest in New York City?"

Angelo nodded. "Yes, sir. My men located two of them near the town of Sant'Antonio Abate."

Mauro stared at the table and then raised his head. "The D'Arco clan. We arrested six of them when we discovered where they were manufacturing the coffee pods filled with cocaine. They're a large group... many Africans and people from the Middle East. Besides drugs and counterfeit products, they're implicated in illegal hazardous waste disposal."

"These three would stick to trafficking drugs." Joe said. "But at the moment, I'd guess they're only thinking about keeping themselves out of an American jail."

"Arresting them will not be easy, Captain Randi."

Angelo looked at Mauro and raised his eyebrows. "We discovered that when we had a window shot of our car."

"I heard. I doubt D'Arco had anything to do with the shooting," Mauro said. "He'll help your fugitives, but he will not lose money because of them."

"What do you mean, sir?" Joe asked.

"D'Arco's not stupid. Shooting at a Carabinieri vehicle only makes us more determined. In the past he's shut down activities to avoid conflict with the police. The three who spent years in New York may not be as accommodating."

Joe focused on the colonel. *He may be right.*

Angelo leaned over the table. "We discovered they may be staying at one of the fugitive's sister's house. I have two men watching the residence. If they are inside, we plan to raid the place."

Mauro looked at him and paused. "I'm not comfortable having your task force running operations in my jurisdiction without the help of my men. Colonel Aldo asked me to give you some leeway, and for the time being I will."

Joe interceded. "Sir. We don't want to put you in an unfavorable position. Colonel Aldo speaks highly of the Naples Command, and we'll do whatever you believe is best."

"Continue on your own, but you'll soon need our help. D'Arco's clan is organized. There are many places to hide the fugitives, and your men are unfamiliar with the area. Be careful."

"We will, sir." Angelo replied.

Joe and Angelo stood when Colonel Ferrara pushed himself away from the table.

"Keep me informed, Captain Randi."

## Chapter XIII

## MARIA'S HOUSE

That night at the safe house, Joe listened to Angelo lay out his plan. They would raid Little Tuna's sister's house in the morning. The key to the operation was to wait for Claudio to tell them if he saw any of the fugitives at the residence.

The next morning, Claudio's call came at eight. Little Tuna had come out, smoked a cigarette, and then went back inside the house.

Thirty minutes later, Sabatino climbed into the Land Rover. He drove. Angelo sat next to him.

Joe took a deep breath. *Hope we have enough men.* He and Gennaro sat in back. Five officers manned the lead vehicle. All the officers wore ominous-looking dark blue tactical uniforms, balaclava full-face masks, and vests with CARABINIERI printed in large white letters on the front and back. Each man carried a holstered Beretta semi-automatic pistol, and an MP5 slung across his chest.

### 

Sabatino slowed the SUV as they approached the house. He waited until the five men in the first vehicle turned into an alley adjacent the residence. Their goal was to secure the back and sides of the house so no one would escape.

Sabatino stopped in front of the single-story house. Joe and the others jumped out of the vehicles and ran to the door.

Gennaro rang the bell and pounded on the steel door frame with a crowbar. "Carabinieri! Open up!" he yelled glancing at Angelo for guidance.

After five seconds with no answer, Angelo nodded.

Gennaro slammed the crowbar into the space near the deadbolt. With a loud crunch the lock popped, and he jumped aside.

Sabatino kicked in the door and Angelo and Joe raced in. Angelo spun from the foyer to the living room and leveled his MP5 on Gino and Maria, huddled in a corner. "Don't move!"

Maria, fell to her knees beside Gino, squatting against the wall, and clamped a hand around her husband's arm. She jabbed a finger at Angelo. "What are you doing?" Tears ran down her cheeks as she turned away from the officers and sobbed.

Gino glared at Angelo and pulled Maria close to his side. "Why are you doing this to us," he yelled.

Joe followed Sabatino, down a hallway to the back of the home. Sabatino opened a door leading to the small yard.

Three uniformed men entered. "Clear each room while Joe and I check on the captain."

Gino and Maria now sat on the couch, their eyes locked on Angelo. She wiped tears from her cheek.

"You people are crazy! We've done nothing wrong!" Gino screamed. "You'll pay to have our door replaced."

Joe wondered if Angelo was smiling under his mask.

"Maybe, but that depends on what we find," Angelo said.

"I told you no one is here. I don't know where my brother-in-law is."

A young officer walked into the room with a grim expression on his face. "You need to take a look at what we found," he said to Angelo.

Angelo looked at Sabatino and pointed to Gino and Maria. "Stay with these two." He and Joe followed the man.

As soon as they entered a bedroom, Joe stopped. He scanned the clean windowless room, furnished with a double bed, and a tall five-drawer dresser. A large crucifix hung on the wall above the dresser. *Something is odd.* He looked to the left at a four-foot-long and three-foot-deep closet cut into the wall. *Never seen an American style closet in an Italian home.* On the floor, outside the closet, lay a brick size chunk of metal with a handle attached.

One officer picked it up and held it in front of Angelo. "It's a strong magnet," he said. He lowered the magnet to the floor at one end of the closet. When the metal came within an inch of the floor, it slammed against the hardwood planks. He pulled and the entire floor of the closet rose.

Joe's eyes widened and he and Angelo moved to the opening. Speechless, both stared at a set of stairs leading below ground.

"Did anyone go down there?" Angelo asked.

The officer nearest him nodded. "I did. It leads to a basement full of junk. There's a locked door framed into a rock wall."

"Follow me, Joe." Angelo motioned to his men. "Two of you come with us."

At the bottom of the stairs, one officer pointed toward the door.

"Where's the crowbar?" Angelo asked.

"With Gennaro, out front," an officer said.

"Get it." Angelo turned to Joe. "A door in a stone wall? Looks odd, doesn't it?"

Joe nodded. "My grandfather had a door in his basement that led to a wine cellar. Made of old solid planks of oak, and he kept it locked to keep the kids out."

"If we find barrels of wine behind this door, I'll buy you dinner tonight."

When the officer returned, everyone stepped to the side and trained their weapons on the door while he crowbarred it open.

Joe and Angelo looked down a stone and brick tunnel that appeared to be thirty feet long.

"Just what I thought." Angelo said. "It's wide and high enough for that fat ass." He motioned for one of his men to lead the way.

At the end of the passageway a set of stairs led up to ground level.

Joe stepped from the stairs into a garage. The door opened to a street behind the Di Napoli house. He and Angelo glanced at a white Fiat parked across the street. The driver's side window was open, but the vehicle appeared to be empty.

Joe turned to Angelo. "They must have gone through the tunnel and had a car in here."

A gun shot reverberated through the garage.

"Jesus!" Angelo grabbed his calf as he fell to the floor.

Joe turned his MP5 toward the Fiat as a pistol pointed at them from the driver's side window. He fired three rounds, and before he could take cover, saw a muzzle flash.

A bullet slammed into his stomach with the force of a professional player's baseball bat. The impact knocked him on his ass. The last thing he heard before hitting the floor was screeching tires, and a long burst from an MP5.

## Chapter XIV

## RETURN TO ROME

Four hours after the raid, Joe stood in front of a bathroom mirror in the safe house. He cringed in pain as he removed his bulletproof vest and then his shirt. He examined the three-inch round bruise on his stomach. Bright red blood pooled just below the skin in the center of the welt. Joe touched it with his little finger and flinched. *Jesus that hurts! I'd be dead if it wasn't for the vest.* He put on his shirt, buttoned it over the ugly wound, and walked to the living room.

Angelo sat on the couch with his injured leg resting on a coffee table. A Carabinieri doctor kneeled in front of him and cut the end of five stitches. "You're lucky it only grazed you." After he bandaged the leg, he turned to Joe. "I'm Doctor Fausto Nepi. I understand you're injured."

Joe unbuttoned his shirt and looked down at the bruise.

The doctor raised his eyebrows. "Does it hurt?" He pressed his finger against the center of the wound.

Joe leapt back. "Jesus! Yes, it hurts! All you had to do was ask."

"Sorry. It will be sore for a while... severe pinpointed trauma." He glanced at Angelo. "Why didn't you go to the hospital?"

"That's a long story about Americans getting shot when they're not supposed to be in the line of fire," explained Angelo.

The doctor's eyes narrowed, and he turned to Joe. "You're an American?"

Joe buttoned his shirt, leaned toward the doctor and lowered his voice. "American and Italian. The American side need not hear about this."

Dr. Nepi sighed and rubbed his temple. "Now I know why Colonel Ferrara sent me here and told me to forget what I saw."

###

Two hours later Angelo hobbled out of the kitchen carrying his cell phone. "Talked to Colonel Ferrara. He's mad as hell."

"At us?" Joe asked.

"No."

"Me?"

Angelo shook his head. "The three fugitives. New York City street thugs. Shoot first, ask questions later."

"What's he going to do?"

"Don't know yet. He said he might put pressure on the D'Arco clan. I told him we're going back to Rome for a few days. What did you do with your vest?"

"Left it in my room."

"Give it to Sabatino. Colonel Ferrara said he'll replace it with a new one."

Joe pulled out his cell phone. "Okay. I need to call Nina. She's going out of town."

Angelo raised a hand. "You won't tell her, will you?"

"Hell no! I'll say I was clumsy, had an accident." He headed to his room, sat on the bed and listened to the ring on the speaker.

"Hi, Joe. Where are you?" Nina asked.

"Still in Naples, but I'll be home tomorrow around noon."

"Damn. I fly to Berlin and then to London tomorrow. I'll be back on a direct flight the next day. Will you be at the apartment?"

"Yes."

"I'm not looking forward to the trip."

"Why?"

"I'm flying with two male flight attendants. Both of them think they're comedians."

"What do you mean?"

Nina sighed. "They like to play games. About an hour ago I got a call. When I answered a guy asked if he was speaking to Nina... I think I recognized the voice. I said yes, and he said 'thank you, see you later', and ended the call."

"Assholes." Joe said. "Tell them your husband isn't a friendly guy."

"I already did, and it worked for a while. I'll remind them again."

"What time will you get back to Rome?" Nina asked.

"Before noon. Meet me at the house for lunch at one."

###

Two days later, Joe stood in his kitchen, cut mortadella and capicola, and placed the slices in the refrigerator. He slit two sub rolls, set them on the counter and looked at his watch. *One fifteen.* He walked to his desk and turned on his computer. *The flight must be delayed.*

He checked his email and signed in to the secure section of the U. S. Embassy web page. He answered the non-classified messages, logged off the site and looked at his watch. *Damn! Two ten, she's over an hour late. What the hell is happening?*

Joe grabbed his cell phone from his pocket and tapped Nina's number. The call went to voice mail. He called Alitalia flight information and waited until a woman answered.

"Good afternoon. I need to find out if Nina Belsogno was on the flight from London that was due to arrive in Rome at eleven fifty-five?"

"Sir, I'm not allowed to give out that information."

He shook his head. "I understand, but she's a flight attendant on that plane, and she's my wife."

"I have no way to verify that."

Joe rolled his eyes. *Everything's a secret.* "Thank you." He ended the call.

On the Alitalia Airlines website he checked the arrival time of flights from London. An empty feeling came over him and adrenalin rushed through his veins as he stared at the entry for the last flight from London. The plane landed on time. *She should have been home by now.* He hit Angelo's number twice.

Angelo answered on the second ring. "Hi, Joe."

"Ang, I need a favor!"

"Sure. What's wrong? You sound worried."

"Nina should have come home at one and she's not here yet. The flight from London landed a little before noon, and Alitalia won't tell me if she was on the plane."

"Stay calm and give me a few minutes. I'll call you right back."

Joe pushed himself away from the desk and walked into the kitchen. He opened a bottle of beer, sat at the table, and stared at his phone, willing it to ring for fifteen long minutes.

When it rang, he jumped. "Yes, Ang, what did you find out?"

Angelo paused and lowered his voice. "The supervisor said a man called and told him he was her husband. He said she couldn't work the flights because she was sick."

Joe's jaw tightened, and he pressed his lips together. "Damn it, Angelo, I didn't make that call! It's a setup. Oh my God! If she didn't take the flights, it means she's been missing for two days."

"Let's stay calm, we'll find out what happened. I'll brief Colonel Aldo."

Joe couldn't calm down, but realized Angelo was right. "I'm going to the embassy to tell the security staff, then I'll meet you at your office."

### 

Joe had spent the last few hours in high gear. At three-thirty, he arrived out of breath at Angelo's office. *I lost it at the embassy. Keep your cool.* "Sorry, I came as soon as I could."

Colonel Aldo and Angelo sat near a coffee table. Joe pulled a chair in front of them and dropped into it.

"What is the U.S. Embassy going to do?" Aldo asked.

Joe couldn't answer that question. The embassy had contacted the National Security Agency and the Central Intelligence Agency for assistance. The means by which they gathered information was classified. "I don't know. The Deputy Chief of Mission and the Security Chief were meeting when I left." He shrugged and looked at the two men.

"I have men examining every frame of the surveillance tapes from the security cameras at the central train station and the one at the gate for that flight," Angelo said. "It'll take a few hours... they'll call us the minute they find anything."

The ring of Joe's phone interrupted them. He held up his hand. "Excuse me, I need to take this. Hello... yes, read it." His facial muscles tensed as he listened. "Damn it! I'm at Angelo's office now. I'll tell them. Let me know if you hear anything else." He hung up, pulled himself together, and shook his head. "The embassy just got an email they can't trace. Nina was kidnapped! The message said they wouldn't harm her if we quit looking for the fugitives from New York."

Colonel Aldo pressed his lips into a fine line and leaned forward. "Anything more?"

Joe took a deep breath and fought to keep his composure. "Yes, sir. They want the Italian government to tell the New York police they will no longer help with the investigation, and they want it printed in the newspaper... la Repubblica. Once they see that, they'll release her."

Colonel Aldo's face turned red. "These Camorra bastards don't tell the Italian government what to do!"

Joe cringed as his stomach twisted. His tongue stuck to the roof of his dry mouth. He spun his wedding band around his finger. "Sir, that's not all they said. We need to think about this before we do anything. You said these bastards are dangerous. Nina is Sofia's cousin. They said if we don't follow their instructions, she will be next."

Angelo jumped from his chair. "I'll kill every damn one of them!" He clenched his fists and turned to his boss. "Joe and I will go to Naples—"

"No you won't," Aldo said. "Both of you are letting your emotions get the better of you. That could get Nina killed. Sit down and listen. I know what we need to do to have her released."

## *Chapter XV*

## *MAURO'S TURF*

The next morning Carabinieri Colonel Mauro Ferrara tugged on his uniform jacket as he walked into Dante D'Arco's large living room. *He'll know how serious we are when he sees me,* he thought.

A sergeant came to attention.

Mauro nodded.

The sergeant pointed to a hallway. "Sir. He's in the room at the end of the hall."

Mauro passed three bedrooms and two baths on his way to the door at the back of the house. He entered a small office and scanned the room. A single pedestal desk and office chair stood near the back wall. Two wooden chairs stood in front of the desk. *A converted bedroom.*

Two Carabinieri officers in tactical uniforms and balaclava masks came to attention when he looked at them.

One held an MP5 pointed at the floor. Mauro nodded, and they relaxed. "Leave us and close the door." He glanced at the sound system on a bookcase against a wall and listened to the music. *Puccini's aria. Pavarotti. At least he likes good music.*

He pulled a chair away from the desk and placed it in front of Dante, sitting on a footstool against the wall. *He's sweating. The biggest set of balls will win.* "Good morning Mr. D'Arco. I am Colonel Mauro Ferrara, Provincial Commander of the Carabinieri. Do you know why I'm here?"

Dante looked at him and hesitated. "No. I've done nothing wrong."

Mauro sat and removed his hat. "Let's not bullshit each other. I'm well aware of your position in the community and guarantee you it's about to become untenable. At this moment ten of my men are at your family's grocery store. It is closed, and will stay closed until they complete their search for drugs and counterfeit products. There is no doubt in my mind they will find something after they examine every product, and every container, in the building."

Dante hands trembled. "Why are you doing this? I'm only a businessman supporting my family."

Mauro cocked his head to the side and smiled. "It's sad you and your family must suffer because the local clan kidnapped an American cop's wife, and threatened a woman named Sofia, the wife of a Carabinieri captain. I would think the members of O Sistema had more brains than to shoot at my men and seize a woman off the street in Rome."

Dante furrowed his brow and rubbed his hands on his pant leg. "I don't know what you're talking about!"

*I have him where I want him.* Mauro stared at him for ten seconds. "Then I cannot help you. When we finish looking at everything you have touched in the past five years... including the fine lace panties in your wife's dresser drawers, the Financial Police will begin. They'll want to see the books for every business you are associated with."

Dante's nostrils flared, and he stood. "Why would I do anything to a woman in Rome?"

Mauro stared at him. *Think you intimidate me?* He remained seated, lowered his voice and pointed at the stool. "Sit down Mr. D'Arco. My men are outside the door. I can arrange for us to continue this conversation through the bars of a cell in my headquarters."

Dante sat, slumped forward, and covered his face with his hands.

Mauro leaned toward him. "At the moment I'm not sure how involved you are, but it won't take long to get the answer. I find it odd that while we are looking for three fugitives in Sant'Antonio Abate, the wife of an investigator helping us is kidnapped. Now our men in Rome are told to stay out of Naples and to cease looking for the three wanted men. The only conclusion I can make is that the men who left New York, like obedient puppies, followed your orders."

"What fugitives are you talking about?" Dante yelled.

Mauro stood. "If you don't know, then our conversation is finished. I promise one thing. It may take me a week, a month, or a year, but rest assured, a long prison sentence is in your future. Should the woman be released unharmed in the next forty-eight hours, I could return my focus to what I was doing yesterday. Then you can continue to provide for your family. If not, plan to spend most of your time speaking with every government agency I can bring down on your ass." Mauro got up, walked to the doorway, stopped, and turned. "One more thing. If you desire more children with your wife or girlfriend, work on it during the next two or three days. After that someone else will play games in the little bush."

### 

By three that afternoon the two men Dante called, after the colonel left, had arrived at his home.

Nico Basso and Dominic Capasso walked into his office with wide darting eyes. Both men glanced around the room before they sat in wooden chairs in front of the desk. They looked at Dante and remained silent.

The clan leader glanced at the scorpion tattoo on Nico's neck and shook his head. "Which one of you decided to kidnap the American's wife in Rome?"

Nico and Dominic glanced at each other. "Both of us talked about it," Nico said. "We thought it would be a good way to get them to quit looking for Dominic and his friends."

"And who threatened the Carabinieri captain's wife?"

Dominic shook his head. "We didn't!"

"Does the name Sofia sound familiar?"

Nico's eyes widened, and he froze. "We didn't know she was married to a captain."

Dante tensed his muscles and ground his teeth. "Don't lie a second time, Nico!"

Dominic shifted to the edge of his chair and waved a hand. "Wait, a minute. No one told me about threatening a woman named Sofia."

Dante tightened his jaw and glared at Nico. "Is that true?"

"Yes." His eyes lowered to the floor, and he took a deep breath.

The old man's face turned red and a pain shot across his chest. Heat flushed through his body and he wanted to be some place else. Anywhere but here with the walls closing in on him. He leaned on the desk and glared at the two idiots sitting in front of him. "I asked you who thought it was a good idea... who decided to go after the two women?"

Nico raised his hand. "I did. The police were close to arresting our friends at Gino Di Napoli's house."

Dante glared at him. *This asshole may cost me my life.* "When you walked into my home did you see my wife cleaning the mess the Carabinieri made?"

"Yes."

"A colonel, not a sergeant or a lieutenant, but a fucking colonel, and his men, just spent hours in my home looking for a reason to arrest me!"

Nico squirmed in his chair. "I didn't think the—"

"I don't give a shit what you think! Has she been harmed?"

"No."

"Where is she?"

"At a farmhouse, outside Rome."

Dante stood and pointed at Nico. "I want her released in the next twenty-four hours, and she better not have a scratch on her body. And one more thing. If anyone touches the other woman, I will feed them their balls. Get out of my house. When it's done, come back to tell me how it went, and it better be good news. Don't call me! I want you to come here and tell me she was released and is in perfect health. Do you understand me?" he yelled.

"Yes," Nico replied in a low voice.

Dante leaned across his desk. "Get out of my house before I get mad."

Nico ran out of the room.

Dominic stood.

Dante raised a hand. "You stay. We have something to discuss."

Dante rubbed his temples to ease the headache as he stared at the man called *Heads*. "You and your friends are a pain in my ass. Do you want to stay in Naples?"

Dominic nodded. "Yes, our families are here."

Dante paused and tapped his fingernails against the desk. "Our friends in New York City do things differently. If you want to continue enjoying the company of your relatives, I suggest the three of you forget everything you learned there."

Dominic eased air from his lungs. "Please don't worry, we will."

"Italy has changed since you left. We don't like to attract attention from the government." Five seconds passed while Dante stared and pondered his decision to help the three men. "How is Little Tuna?"

"He's fine... the bullet didn't hit the bone. It's still in his leg, but the doctor fixed it."

"Where are you staying now?"

"A vacant apartment above a bakery, not far from Caesar's Bar."

Dante stood. "Tell the others everything I said. Should there be one more problem, I will fix it myself."

### 

Later that afternoon Dominic sat on a timeworn couch in a dingy apartment above the Regina Bakery. He shook his head and looked at Little Tuna and The Saint. "You guys wouldn't believe how mad he was. The Scorpion came close to pissing his pants."

Little Tuna rolled his eyes. "The Scorpion," he mimicked in a high-pitched voice. "I call him the fucking bug." He slapped his knee and grimaced in pain. "Son of a bitch! D'Arco better never try to break my balls. I'll step on him."

"Be careful you'll tear those stitches," Santo said. He raised his hands. "Half of these assholes wouldn't last a week with the wiseguys back in the Village. I don't give a shit what D'Arco says, I'm not spending the rest of my life hiding in this shithole. Why does he want the broad released? She's our insurance policy."

Dominic pressed his lips together and raised his eyebrows. "The old man ain't gonna take the heat for us."

"Tough shit if he doesn't like it," Santo said.

Dominic rubbed the back of his neck and sighed. "Don't piss him off, Santo. He didn't get to be the boss just by providing cannolis to the old ladies at his local church."

## *Chapter XVI*

## *AGONY*

Nina, sat on the ground for hours shivering in the cool dampness. A blindfold, soaked with tears, covered her eyes. Ropes secured both hands behind her back and clamped her legs together at her ankles. When she pushed a hand to the floor, her fingers dug into dirt.

She sensed the emptiness but called out. "Hello! Is anyone here?" The sound of the words rang hollow in her ears. *A shed or a basement.* She tried but couldn't push away thoughts of what had happened last year to her roommate Monique. The horrors swirled through her mind. *How did Monique survive what they did?* She couldn't hold back her sobs.

Thoughts of Monique and Omar continued to bounce around in her head. This must be about drugs, but Joe said she shouldn't worry because everyone in the trawler case was out of the picture. Omar was in jail. Monique now worked as a travel agent, and someone had killed Majid in Tunis. *It could be the guy who took Monique to the ship. What was his name? Yassine, that's it! Joe said they never caught him.*

She heard footsteps. *Wooden stairs... two people.* "Who's there?" No response came as the steps got closer.

A hand touched her ankle and someone untied the rope. "Stand up and turn around," a woman ordered.

As Nina struggled to stand, she saw a brief flash of light flicker through the bottom of the blindfold. *A candle.* She took a deep breath through her nose. *Oil, a lantern.*

The woman spun her around, untied one hand, and retied both of them in front of her body. Firm fingers grabbed her arm, digging into the flesh. "This way. When I tell you, step up the stairs," the woman said, pulling her forward.

Nina focused on the woman's voice. *She's from Naples.*

When they reached the top of the stairs, she inhaled fresh air that smelled of flowers. Nina's feet shuffled through dry grass as the woman pulled her. Her heart raced and thoughts tumbled through her mind. The black cloth covering her eyes kept her from seeing anything.

The woman yanked her arm. "Stop," and released her grip.

Nina heard the metallic sound of a door sliding open.

"Get in the van. Reach up and you'll feel the seat," a man said.

*Another one from Naples. It can't be Yassine.* She found the edge of the floorboard with her foot and hesitated. "No!"

Two hands shoved her forward. "Get in!" a gruff voice ordered. "Now, or I'll throw you on the floor."

She pulled herself onto the seat.

"Move over," the man said.

Nina slid to the far side of seat and felt him sit beside her. "Where are you taking me?"

"Shut up and don't move until I tell you."

She furrowed her brow. The door slammed shut, and she listened to another door open and close. The engine started and her head thrust back when the van lurched forward.

During what seemed like an hour drive, she contemplated her fate. *Why are they doing this? Where are we going? Will I ever see Joe again?*

The time spent in a dark space was hellish, but so far no one had threatened or hurt her. No one told her why they seized her on the street in front of the apartment, or what they wanted.

The van stopped, and she felt the man move from her side. The door slid open.

"Get out and be careful. I don't want you to fall." He pulled her hands, and she scooted across the seat.

When she stepped from the van she froze. *Fish! I smell fish. We're near the water or a fish market.* She trembled, and her knees weakened while she listened for any sound. *Nothing, must be night. Please don't put me on a boat.*

The man grabbed her arm and forced her to walk a short distance. *Cobblestones.*

"Stop," he ordered. "Step up and turn around."

She did as he instructed, turned and sobbed. "Where am I?"

"I told you to shut up. Don't press your luck. Reach to the ground and sit."

With her hands still tied together, she eased them toward the ground, and felt damp concrete. She sat and wiped her fingers on her blouse.

"Listen and do exactly what I say." His breath, inches from her face, smelt of stale cigarettes. "I placed something beside you. Sit here and do not move for two minutes, count to one hundred and twenty. We're watching you."

A door on the van closed. The vehicle drove away.

*One, two, three, four.* She paused. *I'm near a port or a fish market. It stinks. Fifty-five, fifty-six, fifty-seven. They're gone, but who's here? Ninety-one, ninety-two. Stop!* She yanked off the blindfold, saw her purse beside her, and realized she was one block from her apartment building.

### 

Joe sat at the kitchen table and poured an ounce of Crown Royal. He stared at the caramel colored liquid, shook his head and half-filled the glass.

After he returned to Rome, he tried to make sense of what happened to Nina, and how he might have prevented it. He tapped the edge of the glass against the table top and glanced at his watch. *Three AM. It's been four days. I need to trust Aldo and the colonel in Naples, but for how long?*

During the last few days he had many conversations about Nina with Angelo and Colonel Aldo. Both men told him that no organized crime group had ever kidnapped a police officer's wife. Even the old Red Brigades, a left-wing paramilitary organization of the seventies and eighties, never targeted family members. In 1981, when they kidnapped U.S. Army Brigadier General James L. Dozier at his home in Verona, they left his wife bound and chained in the apartment.

He recalled Aldo's words. "Colonel Ferrara passed the word to other major clan leaders. He told them the problems they were about to face resulted from D'Arco's stupidity." Then he assured Joe no one would harm Nina, and she would soon be released.

Joe finished half his whisky and checked his watch for the hundredth time. *Three twenty. I hope it works.* In ten years working Witness Security, and during the last five chasing fugitives around the world, he had never sat on the sidelines. He slammed his hand on the table, grabbed the whisky bottle and added more to his glass. *No more sitting on my ass. Tomorrow I rattle cages.*

He jumped when the doorbell to the street entrance of the building rang. "Wrong apartment, asshole." He took another drink. The last thing he wanted was to deal with a person who had forgotten their key and rang his bell to be let him into the building.

The bell rang three more times and Joe pushed his chair back. *Who is this dumb ass?* On his way to the door, he paused at a small table when he saw the Glock pistol. He picked up the weapon, opened the door and walked to the edge of the stairs. As he focused on the landing at ground level, he heard the electronic deadbolt on the door to the street unlock. *Dummy.* He turned back to his apartment and yelled over his shoulder. "Next time use your damn key before you ring the bell!"

"Joe!"

His heart stopped, and he turned. "Nina!"

Nina raced up the stairs before he could process what happened.

His heart pounded as he sprang down three stairs at a time to meet her on the landing.

Tears streamed down her face as she leapt into his open arms and sobbed.

### 

Joe and Nina slept little that night. They spent their time talking about everything that had happened. When she finished, he filled her in on what he had done since he found out about the kidnapping. The two subjects he did not bring up was taking a bullet to the vest and Angelo being shot in the leg. Once both of them calmed down, Joe called Angelo, and Nina spoke with him.

The next morning, on their way to Colonel Aldo's office, Joe wouldn't let Nina leave his side. After what she had told him at the end of their conversation, he realized she needed to slow down and take care of herself. *I need to convince her to quit her job.*

Joe looked at her oversized gray shirt, tight black jeans, and gray heels. *My God, she is beautiful.* "You look nice today... you look nice every day. I don't know what I'd do without you." He kissed her.

She squeezed his hand and laid her head against his shoulder. "After four days without a bath, two hours in the tub last night helped."

When they entered Colonel Aldo's office, Angelo wrapped his arms around her and kissed her cheeks. Aldo pecked one side.

"Angelo told me what you said on the phone last night." Aldo said. "I'm glad you weren't hurt." He motioned toward the couch.

Angelo and the colonel took the two large armchairs on one side of the table and he and Nina sat on the couch facing them.

Aldo looked at Nina and smiled. "I hope you're not planning to work another case with us. The government will have to pay you a salary."

Nina chuckled. "No. There's much less stress at Alitalia." She pointed at the cane leaning against Angelo's chair. "What happened?"

"I sprained my ankle."

"You and Joe need to take better care of each other."

"What do you mean?" Angelo asked.

"The bruise he got on his chest when he slipped and fell against the railing of the stairs. Both of you are clumsy."

Angelo raised his eyebrows and smiled. "I told him the floor was wet."

"Is it still sore?" Aldo asked Joe.

"A little... I'll get over it."

"Good." Aldo said. "I spoke with Colonel Ferrara earlier this morning. I thanked him for what he and his men did. They helped get you released."

Nina took a deep breath and nodded. "The next time you talk to him, tell him I'm sending an expensive bottle of grappa with Joe, and buying myself a bottle of champagne to celebrate."

Aldo grinned and then raised his eyebrows. "We must remain cautious. I'm assigning men to guard your apartment and Angelo's house. Let's hope D'Arco can control his men."

"What did the gang think they would gain by kidnapping me?"

"We believe none of the clan bosses knew about it," Angelo said. "The three America fugitives may have convinced local gang members to take you. Their only demand was for us to stop looking for them."

"That's crazy!" Nina said. "I know you and Joe won't stop looking."

Aldo nodded. "D'Arco and the other clan leaders aren't stupid. People thought they could take matters into their own hands. They may have brought about their own downfall," Aldo said.

Joe's brow furrowed. "What do you mean?"

"D'Arco doesn't want his clan being targeted by law enforcement. He needs to prove to the other bosses he still controls his men. This could start a war between clans. Someone will pay, and I hope you and Angelo can use it to your advantage."

## *Chapter XVII*

## *THE MESSAGE*

Dante D'Arco's driver pulled to the curb and stopped in front of the TRI Electronics store in Torre Del Greco, south of Naples. Dante sat on the right side in the back of the black Audi A6. A short Asian man, with a crooked scar across his cheek, came out of the store, walked around the car, and took a seat next to him.

Dante wasn't comfortable with the little man. People on the street referred to him as The Ghost, but no one called him that to his face.

"Hello, Luca." *Why the hell did he pick an Italian name?*

The man nodded, and Dante handed him a photograph. "His name is Nico Basso, on the street he's called The Scorpion."

Luca paused. "Where and when?"

"As soon as you find him." He slid an envelope across the seat. "The money and my instructions."

"Will I need to call you when it's done?" He picked up the envelope.

"No. Do as I ask, and I'll hear the news."

"I will." The man got out of the car and the driver pulled away from the curb.

Dante had thought twice before he contacted the little killer. No one knew his real name or where he came from in Asia. The man had no loyalty to any clan. He offered his services to gang leaders and clan bosses throughout the Naples area. His fee was as high as his reputation. He never missed his target. Dante leaned toward the driver. "Take me to the church."

"One nearby?" the driver asked.

"No. Go back to Sant'Antonio... Santa Maria la Nova. The priest needs more money for the ladies' cannolis."

###

Colonel Mauro Ferrara walked into his office the next morning at seven. Lieutenant Savio Vasta followed him carrying a folder. Mauro sat at his desk and Savio waited for him to speak.

"Tell me how it happened, Savio."

"At five this morning, two men coming to work noticed a white sheet at the corner of a building two blocks from here. They went to pick it up and saw blood stains. Under the sheet was a body."

"Man or woman?" Mauro asked.

"A man, sir. In his twenties."

"How did he die?"

"A single gunshot to the back of his head. It must have been a small caliber... no exit wound."

"Anything else?"

"Not much, except there's a note." Savio removed three photographs from the folder and handed them to Mauro. "Two pictures of the body and one of the paper pinned to his shirt. The close-up of his face shows a tattoo on his forehead." He set the folder on the edge of the desk. "This is the file on the dead man."

Mauro placed the photos beside each other and stared at them. His brow furrowed. "Why is there so much blood around the tattoo?"

"They cut it off the side of his neck and laid it on his forehead."

"Any idea why?"

"Yes, sir. I believe they wanted to make sure we could identify him. As soon as we saw the scorpion tattoo, we realized it was Nico Basso."

Mauro set the third photo on top of the other two and focused on it.

"We can't figure out what the note means, sir."

The colonel studied the photo of the note. He looked at the lieutenant and grinned. "I understand it, Savio. Leave these."

Savio came to attention, turned, and walked out of the office.

Mauro removed his cell phone, laid it on the desk and dialed a number. He tapped the speaker icon.

"So, we are both in the office early this morning," Aldo said.

"When you reach our age, what more is there to do? I have news for you."

"Good, I hope," Aldo said.

"It is. Remember when I told you about the meeting I had with Dante D'Arco?"

"Yes. The day he denied knowing anything."

"When I walked into his office, music was playing in the background. He was listening to classical opera, Puccini's Turandot... Luciano Pavarotti singing *Nessun Dorma*."

Aldo chuckled. "Good taste, but what's the point?"

"This morning he sent me a note."

"In the mail?"

"No. A dead man delivered it."

"Nothing that dramatic ever happens in Rome," Aldo said. "What did it say?"

"First, I must tell you who delivered the message. We found it pinned to Nico Basso's shirt. He's one of D'Arco's gang leaders. Suffered massive brain trauma when a bullet bounced around inside his skull."

"It must be an important note."

"It is. I'll read it to you. 'Wives and children have no parts in the opera.' I don't think we need to worry about another kidnapping."

Aldo remained silent for a few seconds. "You think Basso had something to do with Joe's wife being taken?"

"I do. We know the guy well... have a thick file on him. Everyone on the street called him The Scorpion... thought of himself as a bad ass."

"Why, The Scorpion?" Aldo asked.

"He had one tattooed on his neck but the killer removed it."

"How do you know?"

"It was sitting in the center of his forehead. I'll send you the photos."

"Only in Naples, Mauro. D'Arco may be safe for a few days, but I'm sending Angelo and Joe back down there. They'll come to see you when they arrive."

### 

Later that morning Joe and Angelo sat in Colonel Aldo's office.

The colonel relaxed in a large armchair on the other side of the coffee table. He slid two typed pages onto the table. "Thank you for the report, Joe. They didn't give her an opportunity to see anything so I understand why she can't tell us much."

"The only time she could move around was when they took her to the bathroom. The woman removed her blindfold, but kept her own face covered so Nina didn't get a good look at her," Joe said. "But she'd make a good investigator."

"Why do you say that?" Aldo asked.

"One day, after she scooted across the floor, the woman came down the stairs and told her she'd tie her to the wall if she moved again." Joe raised his eyebrows. "Although she never spotted a camera, at that moment, she knew they were watching her. I don't know what D'Arco said, but it worked. They dropped her off outside a fish market a block from our apartment."

Aldo grinned. "You're right, she would be a good investigator. Now let's get back to the dead guy they found in Naples."

"Why did they kill him?" Angelo asked.

"D'Arco realized he had to appease Colonel Ferrara. Mauro took men off of other cases and focused on Dante's criminal organization. Sooner or later it would have led to the other clans taking advantage of the situation and moving in on his territory."

"So. D'Arco did the one thing that would protect his organization. He got rid of the man that created the problem," Joe said.

Aldo nodded. "Yes. He's not stupid. The Carabinieri have kept pressure on the clans but rarely focus on one group. There are over a hundred of them with close to seven thousand members. Mauro's men are spread thin trying to watch everyone."

"Let's hope the fugitives get no more help." Angelo said.

Aldo nodded. "We'll see. I told Colonel Ferrara you and Joe would return. Go to his office when you get there. He plans to reduce the pressure on D'Arco and send him a message. He'll tell him we want the guys we're looking for, and he should quit protecting them."

"We'll leave in the morning," Angelo said.

Aldo raised a finger. "One more thing. Colonel Ferrara formed a group of fifteen officers. Five of them will work undercover in the area where the wanted men are hiding. The other ten, and any equipment you need, are available for you to use. Take a small contingent from your task force."

## Chapter XVIII

## LAST RIGHTS

Joe and Angelo met with Colonel Ferrara and coordinated using the colonel's men in the area where officers had seen the three fugitives. After the meeting, they spent the next few days in the safe house outside the city.

Each day, Claudio received updates from the undercover officers, but could provide Joe and Angelo with little information about the fugitives' whereabouts. On the third day he received information they could use. That afternoon, he sat with Angelo and Joe at the kitchen table.

"It happened outside The Saint's mother's home," Claudio said. "At first the officer thought someone in the family had died when a priest came there. A half hour later two men came out and got into a car. He didn't recognize the men but followed them."

"What made him suspicious?" Joe asked. "Something had to draw his attention."

Claudio nodded. "Nothing at first, but then he noticed the one that looked like a priest... you know, dressed in black, didn't have a white clerical collar."

"Did he get a good look at the man's face?" Angelo asked.

"Not initially. He followed their car for twenty minutes until it stopped in front of the Regina Bakery, close to Caesar's Bar. The two men sat there and talked for ten minutes."

Joe's brow furrowed. "Is that when he identified Santo?"

"No," Claudio said. "Our guy walked into the bakery to buy bread and when he came out, he passed the car. As he did, he got a good look at the two men. He's positive... it's The Saint."

"Good work," Angelo said. "What happened next?"

Claudio smiled. "Santo got out of the car and went into a door next to the bakery. We've confirmed it's the entrance to an apartment above the store. It was for rent two weeks ago, but the sign in the window was removed." He opened a folder and slid one page in front of Joe and one to Angelo. "This is the advertisement made by the rental agency."

Angelo and Joe scanned the paper. "Perfect," Angelo said. "A complete description and drawing of the floor plan." He looked at Claudio. "Have everyone here tonight at six for a briefing. We'll hit the apartment at seven tomorrow morning."

Joe got Claudio's attention. "Tell Gennaro and Sabatino to continue gathering information from the undercover officers. We need to know if they leave the apartment tonight."

"And since the apartment is not at ground level, we won't need to worry about a tunnel, and the floor plan doesn't show another exit," Angelo said. "One way in and one way out."

###

The next morning, before leaving the safe house, Angelo checked the men and their equipment. Colonel Ferrara's ten men would use two Land Rovers. Joe and Angelo would ride in a marked sedan driven by Claudio. Everyone wore tactical uniforms, masks and carried an MP5.

Claudio led the vehicles to Regina Bakery. He slammed on the brakes, stopping with the front of the car on the sidewalk between the bakery and the door to the apartment. Two people standing near the bakery entrance ran up the street.

Joe leapt out of the back door as the first Land Rover turned onto a street along the side of the building. The second vehicle stopped next to the sedan and five Carabinieri jumped out. Claudio and the other drivers remained with the vehicles to protect them and keep anyone from approaching the building.

Angelo stood to the side of the door leading to the apartment stairway, turned the knob and pushed. "Locked!" He pointed at an officer. "Break it open."

A large officer stepped in front of the door and another steadied him from behind as he thrust the bottom of his boot against the wood below the handle. The frame shattered, and the door slammed against the stairwell wall.

Two officers slipped past the broken door.

Joe, Angelo and the remaining two men followed as everyone worked their way up the narrow staircase.

An explosion shook the stairway and the walls. Everyone froze and Angelo cringed as he looked to the officer at the back of the line. "Jesus! Find out what happened!"

As the remaining men crept toward the landing, a hand holding a pistol appeared from behind a wall at the open apartment door.

"Gun!" Someone shouted.

Joe dropped and slid up against the wall when he saw the first muzzle flash of three shots. He raised his MP5. *No clear shot, damn it!*

The officer leading the group moaned and pressed himself against the stairs. The man behind him fired six shots toward the door and then turned to his wounded partner. "You okay?"

"Yes. It's my arm, keep going!"

"Get out of here! Claudio will help you," the lead officer said and then turned to Angelo. "He'll be okay. Step over him and follow me."

Angelo and Joe worked their way past the injured officer who held his hand against his blood-stained shirt. At the top of the stairs a pool of blood spread across the floor at the apartment entrance.

"Wait!" Angelo ordered. He pointed at two of his men. "Once we're inside, you two clear one room at a time. Joe, stay with me." He looked at the third officer. "Cover them and watch the other doors along the hallway."

Joe stepped into the living room and kicked a pistol away from Santo, lying on his stomach. Both of Santo's limp arms lay at his side, his face squished against the wall. Joe raised his eyebrows when he saw blood seeping from under the body. He leaned toward the floor. *Damn! Eyes are still open.* He pressed two fingers against the fugitive's neck, but felt no pulse. "He's dead."

Claudio strode into the apartment. "One of those bastards threw a grenade out a window overlooking the side street. The driver and another man were injured. Ambulances are on the way."

Angelo spun toward him. "How bad is it?"

Claudio took a deep breath. "Thank God, the vehicle blocked most of the blast."

"Sir! Come in here!" an officer yelled from a room at the back of the apartment.

Joe followed Angelo into a bedroom where two officers stood next to an open door.

"What the hell is that door doing there?" Angelo asked. "It's not on the plans."

One man pointed. "It's a stairway leading to a vacant storage room at the back of the bakery. A door down there opens to the alley behind the apartment. We checked but saw no one. What happened to the men covering the back?"

Joe shook his head. *These assholes think of everything!*

Angelo glared at the narrow stairway. "A grenade stopped them!" He stomped out of the room. "Come on, Joe. We need to check on our men and talk to the people in the bakery."

Joe tapped him on the shoulder. "One minute, Ang."

Angelo stopped and turned. "I know. This won't work."

Joe nodded. "We need to change our tactics. I have an idea."

## *Chapter XIX*

## *CUT THE CARABINIERI*

After the fiasco at the bakery, Joe could sense Angelo's vile mood.

He stayed out of his partner's way and pondered what had happened since they came to Naples. *Three raids. Lousy results,* he thought. Caesar's Bar turned out to be nothing more than a place for Camorra soldiers to relax and watch soccer. In Little Tuna's sister's house, the tunnel surprised them, and the team left empty-handed. The operation at the apartment above the bakery worried him and Angelo the most. *If they have grenades, they can get larger weapons.*

When he stood in the dingy apartment, and looked down the flight of stairs leading to the storage room, Joe realized the fugitives had an advantage over Angelo's men. Gang members were hard to identify. Task Force officers wore uniforms and drove marked cars. *These guys grew up here... know everyone in town. We're the strangers on the street.*

### 

After the failed raid, he and Angelo sat in Colonel Ferrara's office.

"Thank you for your report. You're lucky none of the three men were seriously hurt," Mauro said. "Tell me about this idea you've discussed."

"Sir. Prior to leaving Rome, Joe and I spent hours talking about the Camorra with Colonel Aldo. After what happened to us here, we thought about the advantages the Clans have over the police in and around Naples."

"In Boston, the Marshals Service faced a similar problem to the one we find ourselves confronted with," Joe said. "We often looked for fugitives in areas we referred to as The Projects."

"Explain the term, projects," Mauro said.

"Groups of government subsidized or low-rent apartment complexes. Many are multi-story... separated by space, a wall or a fence."

Mauro pressed his lips together. "Okay, but that isn't the problem here."

Angelo leaned forward. "Sir. Joe isn't speaking of the buildings, it's the social structure around those complexes that makes our job difficult... almost impossible."

"Explain."

"Gangs control areas." Joe said. "They call it their turf. Many times they use lookouts... even children, to watch for the police or strangers."

Mauro smiled.

"You know where this leads don't you, sir?" Angelo asked.

"Yes, but let Joe finish."

"Thank you, sir. Here we're facing that problem, but on a much larger scale. Clans, with thousands of soldiers, control vast areas in and around Naples. If they have something to protect, they only need to surround it with sentries."

Mauro nodded. "Who report any police in the neighborhood."

"And when they see two or more Carabinieri vehicles together, they know something is about to happen and send out a warning," Angelo said.

"What do you propose we do?" Mauro asked.

"Quit using marked vehicles," Joe said.

"It's a simple fix but also a challenge," Angelo said. "The vehicles can't attract attention. Painting cars and trucks with fake business names won't work. They'd be out of place and the locals would know."

Mauro interrupted by raising his hand. His eyes narrowed, and he glanced around the room. "We'll never get a local business to help us. You need undercover vehicles that the people will accept as commonplace. I think I have an answer to your problem." He walked to his desk, sat and dialed a number. "Good morning. I need information about your repair projects. Is there any cable work being done near Pompeii or Sant'Antonio Abate?" he paused. "Hold on, let me get a pen." He pulled a pad of paper and pen from the side of his desk. "Okay, where?" Mauro scribbled on the pad. "Okay. What work are they doing?" Mauro listened for almost thirty seconds. "Thank you. I'll call you later. Tell your mother I said hello." He ended the call and returned to Joe and Angelo.

Mauro glanced at the notepad. "My nephew, Carlo, is a security manager for Sky Italia. They're upgrading optical cable along the A3 Autostrada east of Pompeii. The D'Arco

Clan controls that area. Let's meet Carlo for lunch near the Archeological Museum. I'll tell him to pick a place."

### 

Joe, Angelo and their men, spent the next four days at a warehouse in Benevento, forty miles northeast of Naples.

"You think this will work?" Angelo asked Joe.

"It depends. The people in and around Sant'Antonio know what Sky Italia is doing. The key to the operation is to make our men look like Sky workers. That means they need to be working on the cable or the junction boxes."

Angelo pressed his lips together and spent a moment focusing on the floor. "When do the two cable workers arrive from Milan?"

"Later today. They're bringing forty sets of work pants and shirts."

Angelo shook his head. "Five people wounded, including us. Remind me to tell everyone to be careful."

Colonel Aldo had arranged for two white Sprinter vans and a smaller Mercedes Viano van to arrive from Rome. It took a day to add Sky Italia graphics to each vehicle.

After inspecting the vehicles, Joe and thirteen officers gathered at a table in a section of the warehouse. Each man held a submachine gun with the stock folded.

Angelo raised a weapon. "The MP5K, with the stock extended, is sixty centimeters." He pressed a lever and folded the stock. "Now it's thirty-seven centimeters." He looked at Joe. "For my American partner that's fourteen and a half inches."

Joe rolled his eyes. "I know."

Everyone chuckled.

Angelo lifted a short canvas sling. "With this sling you can hang it from your shoulder so it rests just below your armpit. Don't celebrate yet. When we finish this operation, these guns go back to the paratroopers of the Tuscania Regiment. Everyone will get gray pants and a Sky Italia shirt baggy enough to conceal the weapon. Make sure you wear a tight undershirt. Keep your vests in the vans." He looked at Claudio. "Did you cover Carabinieri on the front and back of each vest?"

"Yes, sir. With black cloth tape." Claudio pointed to a box on the end of the table. "What's in the box, sir?"

Angelo smiled. "Since we're wearing civilian clothes, we'll need a pistol that's easier to conceal." He pulled a Beretta XP4 Storm Subcompact semi-automatic from the box and held it above his head.

Joe laughed when he heard oohs and aahs from the men. *A bunch of kids waiting for toys.*

"It's small, but it holds thirteen rounds in the magazine and one in the chamber," Angelo said. "Claudio, you have the honor of issuing one to each man. Sadly, I must collect them when we complete the operation."

The prior oohs and aahs turned to boos.

Angelo grinned and shrugged. He removed two folders from the table. "Tomorrow Gennaro will lead one group to the south side of town. Sabatino, your men will cover the north side." He handed the envelopes to the two men. "Divide your groups in half. Rotate taking breaks so they can move around and mingle with the locals. Chief Inspector Costa, Claudio, and I will stay at the safe house. A portable radio, for every two men, is in each van. Keep us informed."

## *Chapter XX*

## *THE WAIT*

By the third day in the safe house, Joe noticed Angelo had become antsy and paced the living room, staring aimlessly at the floor and walls.

Joe shook his head as he sat on the couch watching Angelo trudge from one side of the room to the other. *He's driving me nuts.* He pointed to an armchair. "Ang! Sit down and relax."

Angelo dropped into the chair and raised both his hands. "Nothing. No one has seen them. They're like ghosts."

"It's not as if our men can walk around asking people if they know where these mopes are hiding," Joe said.

"I had my doubts from the beginning."

"What do you mean?"

"Remember what we talked about earlier... central Rome?" Angelo said. "People know their neighbors, their customers, and those who work in nearby businesses. When someone moves into an apartment, or a business hires a new employee, everybody knows it."

Joe shrugged. "It's like that in tight neighborhoods, but what does that have to do with our men?"

"When people in Rome see strangers, they notice them, but think little about it. It's not like that here... the people are different."

"Sure they are," Joe said. "Neapolitans are more family oriented... a closer knit society."

"That's the point, tight-knit, full of mistrust and skepticism. It's worse in a small town like Sant'Antonio Abate. I'll bet half the people are related."

Joe laughed.

"What's funny?"

"You know where my family lives in Italy?"

Angelo nodded. "Yes, Salerno."

"Well, a small town about thirty minutes outside the city... population of about two thousand. Ninety percent of them are my relatives. Let's give it more time, something will develop."

"I hope so." Angelo looked at his watch. "It's seven. That small lunch wasn't enough." He stood. "Let's go for pizza... we'll wear our Sky Italia shirts."

They walked outside and jumped into the white Mercedes van. Angelo drove and turned left at the road in front of the property.

Joe tilted his head back. "Where are you going? There's a place that makes good pizza back the other way."

Angelo looked at him and raised his eyebrows. "Gennaro said the food in *Pizzeria Mezza Luna* was good."

"Are you crazy?" Joe sat up straight in his seat.

"No, but I am bored. Who knows what we may find?"

"What the hell are we going to do if Little Tuna and two of his friends show up for a slice of pizza?"

Angelo shrugged and smiled. "We'll figure something out."

### 

Angelo found a parking space near the pizzeria and they walked into the restaurant. A young waitress, dressed in black slacks and a red shirt, guided them to a table.

*Ten or twelve tables,* Joe thought looking around the room. *Not busy tonight.*

"Would you like wine or coffee?" she asked after they sat.

"Two glasses of the house red wine," Angelo said.

"Water?"

"Yes. Natural, non-carbonated."

She glanced at the letters SKY embroidered on the front of their shirts. "Are you with the men working on the cables?"

Angelo nodded. "Yes, we have two crews in town."

"Both Internet and television?" she asked.

Angelo nodded. "Yes."

The girl jumped. "Good. How fast will the Internet connection be?"

Angelo hesitated.

*Oh shit! Nothing gets past these people.* Joe turned to her. "Once we've installed the fiber cable, we'll offer a speed pack at a reasonable cost... up to three hundred and fifty megabits."

She squealed. "Finally we're getting what they have in Milan."

*Why quit now,* Joe thought. *Make her day.* "There may be other options that are even faster."

The girl giggled. "Everyone will start gaming." She covered her mouth with her hand. "Sorry, back to your order. Would you like pizza or calzone?"

"Pizza Margherita?" Joe asked Angelo.

"No, a Marinara," he said.

Joe smiled at the girl. "One Margherita, and one Marinara." He watched her run to a man standing behind the counter. The young guy pointed at him and Angelo.

Joe caught the waitress's eye and motioned her back to the table.

"Yes. Is there something else you want?" she asked.

"The man behind the counter looked confused. Is there a problem with our order?"

She smiled. "No. He streams movies to his laptop. I told him what you said about new cable."

### 

Emilio had worked in his family's pizzeria since he turned ten years old. After the Second World War, his grandfather opened the business with a loan from the local Camorra boss. Not much had changed over the years. D'Arco's men came to collect his payment on the first Monday of each month.

He snuck glances at the two men from Sky Italia. *I've seen both before, but where?* During the last few days, the only strangers that came in to eat were the men working for the cable company. *They look familiar.*

A customer set a ten Euro note beside the cash register. Emilio took the money and rang up the bill. As he reached for change in the open drawer, his eyes focused on a photo laying on top of the bills. He slid the photo aside and handed the man his change.

Emilio looked at the grainy image of two men and two women standing near a black wall with inscriptions on it. He studied the faces, then took a quick look at the two sitting at the table. His heart fluttered and eyes widened. *That's them!*

Emilio shoved the picture in his pocket and headed to a door leading to the kitchen. On his way, he passed two cooks making pizzas. "I'll be back in a minute." He hurried into the kitchen, pulled out his cell phone and the photo. At the back of the room he leaned against a refrigerator and dialed a number. *Why is everyone looking for them?* "Hi, it's Emilio. Remember the photo you gave me... the two men you wanted to find?" He listened a moment. "They're here in the pizzeria. I recognize them from the picture." He wiped beads of sweat from his forehead and concentrated on the man's voice. "Yes. I'm positive. They're the same guys." He almost dropped the phone when he heard the man's response. "Carabinieri? Hell no! Both work for Sky Italia." He took a deep breath and shook his head. "Okay. The pizzas aren't finished. They'll still be here when you arrive."

When he left the kitchen he saw two more men wearing Sky Italia shirts talking with the two seated. *If he's right, they're all cops.* His eyes widened, and he stopped breathing. *I hope nothing happens in here!*

### 

Sabatino surprised Joe when he and one of his men walked into the pizzeria. After a brief conversation, they ordered slices of pizza and left.

Angelo shook his head. "Still nothing! Where are these guys?"

*I wish he'd relax,* Joe thought. "Don't get discouraged. Sooner or later someone will see them. You can't miss the fat guy."

The waitress brought their pizzas and refilled their glasses with wine from a carafe. "Can I get you anything else?"

"No," Angelo said.

The girl slid the bill on the table and walked away.

Both men remained silent as they dug into a slice.

"I must admit the best pizza in Italy is made in Naples," Angelo said.

"You can thank Raffaele."

Angelo frowned. "Who the hell is he?"

"The guy that made the first Margherita pizza in honor of the Queen Consort of Italy."

Angelo rolled his eyes. "How do you know this shit? What Queen Consort?"

"Margherita Maria Teresa Giovanna," Joe said with a smile.

"Oh, The wife of King Umberto the first. She's buried in the Pantheon in Rome. I forgot the story."

Both of them were laughing when Joe saw Little Tuna's brother-in-law, Gino, walk through the door and stop at the counter. *Jesus, Joe, don't react.* He looked at Angelo, quit smiling, and raised his eyebrows. "Don't turn now, Ang. Gino Di Napoli just walked in... he's at the counter."

"You sure it's him?"

"Yes."

Gino asked for coffee and headed to a table against the back wall. He took a seat facing Angelo and Joe.

Angelo, sitting with his back to Gino, leaned across the table. "Maybe he wanted a coffee. Quite a few locals come here." He looked into Joe's eyes. "I'm glad we were wearing masks when we raided his house. There's no way he could recognize us."

"We've got to ignore him," Joe said. "You think he's waiting for Little Tuna or Dominic Capasso?"

"Could be. Did you bring your weapon?"

Joe nodded and widened his eyes. "Yeah, the Storm... wish it was the MP5."

"Let's take our time, eat, and see what happens."

The waitress took an espresso and a glass of water to Gino's table.

Joe caught glimpses of Gino watching them. "He keeps looking this way."

"Now you're worrying," Angelo said.

Five minutes later Gino got up and strolled out the door without a glance their way.

They finished their meal, paid the bill, and left.

On the way back to the safe house Angelo wouldn't stop talking. "I can't believe it. The first time we go there, someone involved in the case decides he wants a coffee. I'll tell Claudio to coordinate with both crews and have people go the pizzeria more often."

"Good idea," Joe said, "but don't overdo it. They may get suspicious."

"No. All they need to do is rave about the pizza being the best in Naples. Everyone will love them."

## Chapter XXI

## THE WAIT ENDS

Gino pulled to the side of the road before he reached his house. He picked up the photo on the seat next to him and studied the image of two men and women in New York City. *It's them. The captain and the American cop.* "I bet they're the bastards who came to my house." *Better call Little Tuna.* He yanked his cell phone from his pocket and dialed.

"Francesco, it's me. Emilio was right. They're the two cops in the photo. I arranged for two kids on motorcycles to follow them when they leave the restaurant. One of them will call me later and tell me where they went." He listened to his brother-in-law and frowned. "Give them a hundred Euros? They're teenagers... that's too much." He pulled the phone from his ear when Francesco yelled. After Francesco stopped shouting, Gino shook his head. "Okay, okay! I'll call and tell them. It's your money. You want me to call the boss?"

Gino cringed when his brother-in-law screamed again. He held the phone six inches from his ear and let him finish his rant. "Yes, I know you don't like him. I won't tell anyone."

### 

Twenty-four hours after they saw Gino, Joe and Angelo had made arrangements with their men to spend more time in *Pizzeria Mezza Luna.* Angelo told Sabatino to move his team from the north side of town to a large cable junction box closer to the restaurant.

Joe noticed Angelo was more relaxed and confident as they waited for someone to report seeing the fugitives. Joe occupied his time answering emails from the embassy and from Nina.

At eleven that night, both of them sat on the living room couch and watched the late international news on the RAI News 24 channel. Joe finished cleaning his Beretta Storm and reassembled the pistol. He checked the 9mm rounds in the magazine and shoved it into the weapon. Chambering a round in the pistol, he set it next to his leg.

A newspaper on the coffee table caught his eye. He picked it up, saw it was a day old, and tossed it on top of the Beretta.

Angelo's head nodded. He yawned and rubbed his face.

"Tired?" Joe asked.

"A little. Waiting for something to happen is driving me crazy."

Joe laughed. "Me too. The embassy Deputy Chief wants to know what the hell I'm doing down here."

"You didn't tell him, did you?"

"Hell no. I'm getting good at stretching the truth. Told him we were helping the Naples Command setup a mini task force to catch the fugitives."

"You think he'll believe you?"

Joe shrugged. "Sure. Typical ass-covering politician. Hasn't seen me for over a week and needs something to tell the ambassador should he ask."

Angelo's cell phone rang. "Hello." He paused and listened. "Okay, Joe and I are both awake. We'll see you in a few minutes."

"Who was that?"

"Claudio. He's on his way. He and his men will start again at seven in the morning."

"What about Gennaro and Sabatino?" Joe asked.

"They won't come for at least a half hour." Angelo headed to the kitchen. "Want anything?"

"No thanks."

Angelo returned with a bottle of water and set it on the coffee table just as the doorbell rang. "Who the hell is that? I didn't hear a car. I'll bet Claudio forgot his key."

Joe shrugged. "Might have, he's got a lot on his mind."

Angelo grinned, walked to the door and yanked it open.

Joe froze when Little Tuna barged in with a revolver pointed at Angelo's head. He forced Angelo back into the room.

"Don't do anything stupid, Captain Randi," the fat guy said.

Joe didn't have time to react before a skinny guy ran in and pointed a gun at him.

"Don't move!" the kid yelled.

Joe raised both his hands to chest level. *Holy shit! We're in trouble.*

Little Tuna pointed at the couch. "Sit with your American friend," he ordered.

*How the hell does he know who we are?* Joe tightened his jaw. *Well, they knew about Nina.*

Francesco and his friend stepped back and looked at them.

Francesco lowered the revolver to his side. "Both of you have been causing a lot of problems. Who shot Santo?"

Joe answered. "We didn't. Must have been someone from another clan."

"Sure, guys on the street in Carabinieri uniforms. I'm not that dumb."

Joe stared at him. *Yeah, fat ass, whales are smart.* His muscles tensed and he eased his hands to his lap. *Be careful, this guy is dangerous.*

"What do you want?" Angelo asked.

"For both of you to disappear... forever. No way am I going back to New York to be locked in an American shit hole."

"It's better than sitting in an Italian jail," Angelo said. "We can help you get a reduced sentence."

Francesco laughed. "You're not listening. I don't plan to see the inside of any jail. In a few weeks, I'll fly to Canada, get a new name, and then cross the border." He turned to his accomplice. "See if they have wine in the kitchen... we'll toast their departure."

Angelo placed both his hands on his thighs.

*Does Ang have his pistol?* Joe wondered.

"Every police officer in Italy will look for you," Angelo said. "There's no way for you to escape."

Little Tuna laughed. "We already made plans. Dominic and I will be in Albania in a few days. The police can waste their time searching every house in Italy."

*Doesn't look good. He's giving up too much information.* Joe bit his lip. *The bastard's gonna kill us.*

Francesco looked toward the kitchen. "What the hell you doing, making the wine?"

"There are no clean glasses!" his partner yelled.

Little Tuna took a deep breath and stared at the door to the kitchen. "Just bring the damn bottle!"

*Now! It's my only chance,* Joe thought. He glanced at the newspaper, moved his hand to his side and slid it under the paper. In one swift motion he wrapped his hand around the pistol grip, raised the weapon, and fired two shots into Francesco's chest.

The big guy staggered back. His bulging eyes locked on Joe as he raised his pistol.

Joe fired a third shot, hitting the fugitive in the center of his throat. Francesco grabbed his neck and blood spurted through his fingers.

Shouting came from the kitchen. "Francesco, you okay?"

Joe jumped from the couch.

Little Tuna floundered, flailed his arms, and fell, with a loud thud, to the floor.

Angelo leapt from his seat, knocking the coffee table aside. He dove to the pistol clutched in Tuna's hand.

"Francesco!" The skinny guy screamed as he bolted through the kitchen doorway with his gun held in front of him. His face contorted when he saw Tuna on the floor. He pulled the trigger as he swung the weapon toward Angelo.

Bullets whizzed over their heads.

Joe dropped to one knee and raised his Beretta with both hands. He fired three shots into the man's chest.

"Jesus!" Angelo yelled.

Joe approached the body sprawled on the floor outside the kitchen. He figured the guy was dead but touched his neck to check for a pulse.

Angelo stood over him. "Christ, I thought we were dead! Where did you get the gun?"

"After I cleaned it, I laid it on the couch. It was under the newspaper. Almost forgot it was there." Joe took a deep breath and exhaled. "The next time we pass a church, we'll stop and light candles."

Angelo placed a hand on Joe's shoulder. "I'll never forget this."

"Neither one of us will." Joe pointed at Little Tuna's body. "That bastard made up his mind, we were both going to die."

Angelo pulled his cell phone from his pocket. "I'll call Colonel Ferrara. You call Gennaro and Sabatino. Tell them to bring their crews here as soon as possible."

Joe's muscles tensed, and he glanced around the room. "Why wasn't Dominic with him? If more of them are outside, they had to hear the shots!"

"Damn!" Angelo's eyes widened. He raised the twenty-two caliber pistol he had taken from Little Tuna. "This thing is worthless." He threw it on the table. "Give me your Storm and get two submachine guns. I'll lock the door and close the windows. We have the advantage as long as we stay in the house."

Joe handed him the Beretta.

"How many rounds are left?"

"Seven." Joe bolted down a hallway.

When he returned, he held an MP5 and a small canvas bag in each hand. *Angelo's been busy.* An oversized armchair blocked the front door. The couch, with the coffee table turned over on top of it, sat to the side of the room. He handed Angelo a weapon and bag. "There are six extra magazines in the bag."

"Did you make the calls?"

"Yeah." Joe chambered a round in the MP5 and removed the magazines from the bag. "Claudio is five minutes from here. The rest of them will take a half hour or more."

"Did you tell them what happened?"

Joe raised his shoulders and eyebrows. "Only that we had a one-sided gun battle with Francesco, and he lost. Claudio will park down the road and check if anyone is near the house. When he meets the others, he'll send me a text. What about Mauro?"

"It will be over an hour before he and his men arrive." He walked to Joe and shook his head. "He would have taken a drink of wine and pulled the trigger."

The words made Joe shudder. *He's right!* Little Tuna didn't worry about the ramifications. He and Dominic may have gotten out of the country, but someone would have found them. *We wouldn't be there to see it.*

## Chapter XXII

## BORING TRIP

Two days later, Joe, DEA Agent Paul Sacca and FBI Agent Robert Duffy sat in Angelo's office in Rome.

"Now that Dominic Capasso turned himself in, tell us what happened," Paul said. "We heard there was a shootout."

"One of my men shot The Saint, Santo Esposito, when we raided an apartment in town. He died before we got to him," Angelo said. "Francesco Russo, Little Tuna, and Dominic, got out by going down a hidden flight of stairs."

Duffy furrowed his brow. "Little Tuna was the fat guy, right?"

Joe nodded. "Yeah. The reincarnation of Mimos, the giant."

Duffy tilted his head to the side and looked at the three men. "Mimos? Who the hell is he? I thought you were only looking for three men?"

Joe smiled at Duffy. *You can't help liking this guy.* "Mimos is the mythological giant buried under Mount Vesuvius."

"Oh! Never read that story," Duffy said. "So you refer to Little Tuna as a giant?"

"If you saw him you'd understand. He was that big," Angelo said.

"The first time we got close to them, one of our men put a bullet in Francesco's leg," Joe added.

"Any of your men get injured?" Paul asked. He looked at Angelo. "You were limping, and Joe said he bruised his stomach."

Angelo didn't wait for Joe to answer. "Nothing bad... small accidents. A few of my men took fragments... Joe and I are clumsy."

"So, Francesco is dead. How did that happen?" Duffy asked.

"He showed up at the wrong place with a pistol. An officer on the task force shot him," Joe said.

Angelo stood. "That's it. When we finish writing our report we'll send you both a copy."

Paul and Robert left the office.

"We can't give them the same report we're writing for Colonel Aldo," Angelo said.

"I know. If the Ambassador finds out everything, he'll tie me to my desk."

Angelo headed to his desk. "Let's get started. We meet with Colonel Aldo the day after tomorrow."

## *Chapter XXIII*

## *THE GIRLS*

That night Joe, Angelo and their wives finished dinner in the candlelit downstairs dining room at the Target Restaurant.

Sofia looked at both men. "I'm glad you don't need to go back to Naples. Nina and I are tired of being alone and having guards watch us twenty-four hours a day."

"Did you catch all the men you were looking for?" asked Nina.

Joe glanced at Angelo and smiled. During the two-hour drive back to Rome, they discussed what they would tell the women. They both agreed there was no reason to bring up what had happened at the safe house. "Two of them gave us no problem when we took custody of them. A day later, the third guy turned himself in to the Carabinieri."

Sofia turned to her husband. "When can we get rid of the guards around the house?"

"Joe and I spoke with Colonel Aldo. They won't be back tomorrow."

"What about our apartment?" Nina asked Joe.

"Don't worry. Today's the last day. The asshole that planned your kidnapping is no longer a free man. The people who held you were threatened with the same fate."

"I hope you'll both be spending more time at home," Sofia said to Angelo.

"We will."

Nina smiled at Joe. "Sofia and I want to go to Saturnia's thermal baths." She glanced between Angelo and Joe. "Will you take us?"

Joe raised his eyebrows. "The hot springs in Tuscany. The water is a hundred degrees."

Sofia raised a finger. "And we want to stay at the Wellness and Spa Center... at least three days."

Joe looked at Angelo. "You ever been there?"

"No, but I heard the Center is luxurious, and exclusive."

"We won't let either of you say no," Nina said.

Sofia pointed at her husband. "You and Joe have been enjoying yourselves running around Naples and eating good pizza and Neapolitan pastries. Now it's time you both work hard to please your wives."

Angelo grinned. "Okay. When we meet with Colonel Aldo, I'll ask him for a week vacation. I'm sure Joe can get away from the embassy for a while."

## Chapter XXIV

## TELL US

After Colonel Aldo returned from a trip to thank his friend Mauro, Joe, Nina and Angelo met him in his office. He had asked Joe to bring his wife so they could further discuss what had happened while being held.

Angelo convinced him to not to mention his and Joe's injuries.

"Did you get a good look at the people when they took you?" Aldo asked Nina.

"No. I came out of my apartment building and two men behind me grabbed my arms. They put a black cloth bag over my head and shoved me into a van."

"Are you sure it was a van?" Angelo asked.

"Yes, a white one. I saw it parked in front of the door when I walked out."

Aldo nodded. "Then what happened?"

"We drove for a long time... at least an hour. When we stopped, they took me to a room down a flight of stairs. They removed the cover from my head, but I didn't see a thing. There was no light in the room. Someone wrapped a dark cloth across my eyes and tied my hands and feet."

"Could you tell what direction they drove?" Angelo asked.

"No. I couldn't see through the cloth. While in the room, no one talked, but someone put a water bottle to my lips and allowed me to drink. They didn't give me anything to eat the first day. I sat there for the longest time, lowered myself to the dirt floor and fell asleep. After that, they gave me a bowl of pasta and chicken each day."

"Are you sure the floor was dirt?" Aldo asked.

"Yes. I dug my fingers into the soil."

"Based on what she told me, it may have been the basement to a house," Joe said.

Nina looked at him and nodded. "It was damp and smelled musty."

The conversation continued, but Nina provided scant details. She didn't realize how long they held her, but later found it was for four days. She couldn't tell them much about her captors, except for their accents.

A tear rolled down her cheek. "All I thought about was what happened to Monique on that ship. Can we continue this later?"

"There's no need to," Aldo said. "We have Joe's report. If you think of anything more, tell him."

Nina pulled a tissue from her purse and dabbed her eyes.

Joe stood and helped her to her feet. He wrapped his arms around her waist, then stepped back and looked into her eyes. "You better tell them what else has happened."

Angelo and Aldo stood.

Angelo took her hand. "Is it important?"

Nina nodded. "Yes."

"We need for you to tell us where, when and how it happened. Every detail is important," Aldo said.

Nina stared at him. "I'm sorry but I can't give you the exact details, but I know how it happened."

"Try to do the best you can," Aldo said.

Nina raised both her hands and her eyebrows. She took Joe's hand and squeezed it against her chest. "I'm pregnant!"

THE END

www.ingramcontent.com/pod-product-compliance
Lightning Source LLC
Chambersburg PA
CBHW050125280326
41933CB00010B/1244